THE ROBBER BARONS REVISITED

Problems in American Civilization

The

ROBBER BARONS

Revisited

EDITED WITH AN INTRODUCTION BY

Peter d'A. Jones

SMITH COLLEGE

D. C. HEATH AND COMPANY · Boston
A division of RAYTHEON EDUCATION COMPANY

Library of Congress Catalog Card Number: 68-19011

INTRODUCTION

AMERICA'S business leaders of the late nineteenth century have been called "Robber Barons" for so long now that the label is never likely to disappear. The phrase used frequently to describe the 1880's and '90's, the "Gilded Age," comes directly from Mark Twain; the first adoption of the "Robber Barons" tag is less certain. E. L. Godkin, the editor of *The Nation,* used the phrase "medieval barons" as early as 1869; Henry Demarest Lloyd picked up or re-coined this idea in 1882; and another journalist, Carl Schurz, used the very words "Robber Barons" in a Harvard speech of the same year. Lloyd, Thorstein Veblen, W. J. Ghent (*Our Benevolent Feudalism,* 1902), and the English economist J. A. Hobson, among others, gave the phrase greater currency. It is so familiar today among students of American history that the original meaning of the phrase, or at least of its adjective, has become diluted. We tend to talk of "Robber Barons" when we simply mean "big business leaders" of a specific era, the Gilded Age.

Does this situation reflect a longstanding ambivalence of Americans towards big business in general? As Thurman Arnold wrote in 1937 of the trusts led by the so-called Robber Barons, ". . . the antitrust laws were the answer of a society which unconsciously felt the need of great organizations and at the same time had to deny them a place in the moral and logical ideology of the social structure." (*The Folklore of Capitalism,* p. 211.) Why this ambiguity? Partly because the Robber Baron and the corporation — as driver and engine — helped to create both material progress and social dislocation. The new industrial, urban way of life was constructed only by making the old commercial and rural way derelict; the new large-scale organizations were introduced only at the expense of the family firm and the small partnership. The ambiguity of Americans towards this two-sided process was thus built-in and historical.

The Industrial Revolution came to the United States in the 1840's and '50's via New England, where the factory system was established in the textile trades. Whether the Civil War helped or hindered the spread of that economic revolution is still a matter of dispute among historians. But the transcontinental railroad was completed in 1869, and the Republican Party did manage to erect a virtual one-party system for many years, giving the American businessman everything he needed, or thought he needed — protective tariffs, a national currency and banking system, liberal land-grants to private corporations, and freedom from taxation.

In such a favorable political system a generation of business leaders, the "Robber Barons," rose to preeminence as masters of great railroad networks and large manufacturing corporations. With astonishing rapidity they mapped out and constructed America's productive framework. Down to the 1890's they could find support in the popular philosophy of the day — conservative Social Darwinism, which lauded the "survival of the fittest," and the Gospel of Wealth, which rationalized inequality and was preached with conviction from leading church pulpits throughout the land. By the middle of the twentieth century the corporation had surpassed its creators, and the era of the great individual "captain of industry" was over — the Corporate Age had replaced the Heroic Age of American business. But between the Civil War and the First World War the Robber Barons directed crucial growth sectors of the American economy and could wield great personal power, if they so wished.

The reactions of Americans who lived in the Robber Baron years were conflicting. This is seen clearly in the diametrically opposed writings of Henry Demarest Lloyd and Edward Atkinson. Lloyd, the precursor and classic model for the "Muckraking" journalists of the Progressive era, has no doubts about the entrepreneurs of the Gilded Age: these "Lords of Industry" are evil monopolists and profiteers. Atkinson on the other hand, a highly successful inventor-businessman and spokesman for policies of *laissez-faire,* asserts that the great capitalists created wealth, and in their search for efficiency in production they made all Americans better off. "Did Vanderbilt keep any of you down by saving you $2.75 on a barrel of flour, while he was making 14 cents?" he asked pointedly in 1886. Atkinson and Lloyd set the scene in general terms for the long-lasting public debate on the question, "The Robber Barons — industrial pirates or industrial pioneers?"

Over the years Edward Atkinson's argument has been indirectly supported by the American belief in rags-to-riches. If American society offered ample opportunity for young men of poor origins to make their fortunes, then why should Americans condemn the successful? Henry Demarest Lloyd's argument, though, was that the Robber Barons *monopolized* the channels of economic opportunity and deliberately blocked the roads to success for those who tried to come after them. What evidence is there for either of these visions of American history in the late nineteenth century? Was there in fact a loss of opportunity in these years; did upward social mobility slow down? Or is there plenty of evidence for rags-to-riches? Andrew Carnegie presents a classic example of the poor-boy-makes-good story, by describing his artisan, radical, immigrant background in simple but telling terms. A recent economic historian, William Miller, after studying the origins of a given number of business leaders in this period, shows that the bulk of them came from white Anglo-Saxon Protestant, urban, Northeastern, educated professional and business families. Apparently the doors of business success were not easily opened to immigrants, farm boys, or youths of poor education and background. Does William Miller's historical evidence reduce the rags-to-riches idea to a myth in American history? Was Carnegie merely a special exception? In any case, do the social characteristics of business leaders in general, as in-

vestigated by Miller, coincide with those of the Robber Barons in particular? Even Matthew Josephson, the sharp business critic of the 1930's, admits in his study of a dozen or so Robber Barons that all were poor in childhood (except J. P. Morgan, whose father was a banker) and that all left home when young to make their fortunes.

Whatever their social origins, the entrepreneurs came in for a barrage of accusations. Both in their own day and since, they have been charged with industrial piracy of various sorts. These accusations include financial tricks such as cornering and watering stock; political corruption and the bribing of legislatures; inhumanity to labor through the imposition of heavy hours, peremptory wage-cuts and lockouts, the suppression of trade unions by fair means and foul, and the use of cheap immigrant contract labor to undercut wage-rates and defeat strikes; disregard for the American consumer and the fixing of monopoly prices. Above all, they have been condemned for ruthless competition — choking off rivals by use of railroad rebates and drawbacks, control of raw material supplies, industrial espionage and other devices culminating in forced purchase of competitive firms. The historical literature is too rich to illustrate all these indictments in one book of readings, but some of the major charges are brought out in Part Three of this volume, "The Robber Barons as Industrial Pirates."

Three major industries are used in Part Three to exemplify the charges of industrial piracy against American business leaders (railroads, oil, and sugar-refining); and three industries reflect in Part Four the pioneering aspects of business leadership (steel, meatpacking and electronics). Lord Bryce, whose influential work on the U. S. political system, *The American Commonwealth* (1888), was widely read in this period, gives an excellent short description of America's railroad kings. Bryce focusses attention on the first industry to be accused of "piracy." Among the railroad "pirates," Jay Gould stirred up the most enmity and the least support from contemporaries and from later historians. Matthew Josephson's portrait of Gould as an evil Mephistopheles (written in 1934, a year when American businessmen were scarcely at the height of their popularity) is a standard exposé of the "Muckraking" type. Gould emerges as an unscrupulous and shady empire-builder, manipulating and watering stock, deliberately running businesses down and building them up again to his own advantage. For most people Jay Gould remains the archetypal corrupt railroad king of the Gilded Age. But in 1957 the late Julius Grodinsky took a different line in a scholarly, temperate, revisionist biography of Gould. Grodinsky sees his subject as a "business type," an entrepreneur with human virtues as well as human vices, working at corporate finance in a period of history when little was known about scientific financial practices and when corporate law was still primitive. Despite his faults, Gould taught his countrymen how to amass capital for large-scale investment; he built many miles of track, and reduced railroad rates for the American public. Julius Grodinsky is careful to admit some of the misdeeds cited by Matthew Josephson and other critics of Gould. Does his evidence and presentation force us to adopt a new picture even of Jay Gould, long-regarded as the prototype Robber Baron?

If the railroad industry produced the first "kings," the oil industry attracted the most public attention, perhaps because the oil refiners sold a consumer product that went into every American home — lighting oil. The most common allegation against corporate leaders was that they employed trickery against competitors and smaller businessmen in the same field, especially using their large buying-power to demand "rebates" and "drawbacks" from common carriers — the railroads — to gain crippling advantages over their rivals. Henry Demarest Lloyd, who spent a good deal of his time investigating John D. Rockefeller and the activities of the Standard Oil Company, describes the South Improvement Company scheme as a "fiendish conspiracy" by Rockefeller to persuade the railroads to destroy his competitors in the oil business by charging them high freights, by giving Standard Oil lower freights ("rebates"), and even by paying back to Standard Oil the margin of excess freights paid by its rivals ("drawbacks"). In Lloyd's account, the Company wielded its monopoly power to the detriment of small businessmen and the general public.

Many years later, however, the revisionist biographer of Rockefeller, Allan Nevins, sees the South Improvement Company plan merely as the natural response of businessmen in an impossibly competitive field to adverse and fluctuating trade conditions. Rockefeller is pictured by Allan Nevins as a man concerned less with local rivalries between oil refiners and railroads than with fear of what general trade depression (caused by over-competition) could do to *all* the manufacturers. Moreover, in a later section of the same biography (first published as early as 1940), Allan Nevins shows that some of the so-called "small businessmen" destroyed by Rockefeller were either financially able to look after themselves, and simply lost out in the tough battle for the oil fields, or were little less than blackmailers, who consciously entered some area of business activity in which they knew Standard Oil was interested, in order to be bought out at a good price. Were these people victims or blackmailers? The evidence suggested by Lloyd's *Wealth Against Commonwealth* (1894) or Ida M. Tarbell's *History of the Standard Oil Company* (1904) stands out in sharp contrast to the material collected and interpreted by Professor Nevins.

Sugar-refining was another industry in which the public interest was directly involved through the home. The price war in the sugar industry was particularly tough. When a House of Representatives Committee investigated the "Sugar Trust" (legally, the Sugar Refineries' Company) in 1887, the deed of incorporation was presented as evidence. The deed states as among its objects the pursuit of reduced production costs through the pooling of technical resources, the lowering of consumer prices to a level "consistent with reasonable profit," and "protection against unlawful combinations of labor."

Does a careful reading of this seemingly frank document reveal anything "sinister" or "piratical" about the Sugar Trust? When the industry was again investigated, this time by the federal government (the U. S. Industrial Commission), H. O. Havemeyer and other business leaders presented the picture of sugar refineries struggling to survive in a highly competitive field — not unlike Allan Nevins' picture of the oil-refining industry. Their testimony, published in 1900, gives us valuable firsthand details on the price war and the producers' combination movement which sprang up to counter it. Havemeyer was very revealing about his attitude to would-be competitors and to the general public; he did not "care two cents for your ethics," and the job of his company, as he saw it, was to maintain production levels at all costs, to see that rivals did not stay in business too long, and to keep prices as high as possible. In practice, however, Havemeyer claimed, competition was so bitter and the technical efficiency of big firms so superior that consumer prices would fall consistently. Such an argument did not satisfy the socialist writer Gustavus Myers, whose well-known *History of the Great American Fortunes* was first published in 1907. Myers condemns out of hand Havemeyer and his associates in the sugar-refining industry. They were guilty, says Myers, of corrupting politics, of raking in "inordinate profits," and of actually defrauding the U. S. Treasury of thirty million dollars over a twenty-year period by juggling customs rates. Does Myers' evidence meet the arguments presented by the businessmen themselves in their testimony to the U. S. Industrial Commission? Or does it shift the ground of the argument too much (to one of criminal fraud) and thus fail to respond adequately?

The defense of the Robber Barons as creative industrial pioneers is nowhere more clearly stated than in the economist E. S. Meade's account of the innovations for which Andrew Carnegie was said to be responsible in the American steel industry. Writing in the *Quarterly Journal of Economics* in 1901, Meade describes with great clarity the rise of the Carnegie Company and ascribes its success to good organization and integration, swift adoption of new technical innovations and the ploughing-back of profits into the company. Carnegie was ahead, he asserts, because he pioneered and anticipated his rivals; his firm was "the acme of productive efficiency." In total contrast is the view of Andrew Carnegie's ex-literary helpmeet, J. H. Bridge, whose *Inside History of the Carnegie Steel Company* (1903) belittles Carnegie as a business leader. According to Bridge, Carnegie was a lazy, overcautious man who was very slow to take advantage of any new idea in steel or bridge production and whose greatness (like Napoleon's) was but the greatness of his generals. Just as Rockefeller was said by other critics to depend on his associates (H. H. Rogers, J. D. Archbold, S. V. Harkness, Samuel Andrews, H. M. Flagler and others), Bridge argues that Carnegie depended on the talents of his steelmaker, Captain Bill Jones; on the abilities of America's leading coke producer, H. C. Frick; on the financial genius of Henry Phipps, and on the later boss of Bethlehem Steel, C. M. Schwab. Such an attitude is perhaps a natural one for Carnegie's ex-ghost writer to take. Is his argument convincing, when placed against the evidence offered by E. S. Meade? J. H. Bridge sees Carnegie as the very opposite of a risk-bearing "captain of industry," and takes pains to quote his master's famous statement, "Pioneering don't pay!"

In his own autobiography, Carnegie admitted freely that his special genius was not so much technical as organizational. Some other business leaders of the period felt the same way: John D. Rockefeller for instance, openly confessed as the secret of his success, "We had a group of strong men from the outset." Does such an admission make the Robber Barons any less "industrial pio-

needs"? In the world of industry and business, "pioneering" can be defined in many ways. It can range from actual technical *inventions* to all types of *innovations* — the application of new ideas in management, financing, planning, production, labor relations, selling, and advertising. The innovation may be an oil tank-car (which has been called "John D. Rockefeller's Secret Weapon"), or the introduction of mail-order selling (begun by Montgomery Ward in Chicago in 1872). E. S. Meade claims *technical* innovations for Carnegie; J. H. Bridge denies them; and Carnegie himself claims only organizational ability.

A clear historical example of technical innovation in an industry, combined with what has been generally accepted as a clear case of "Robber Baronism," occurs in meat-packing. Charles Edward Russell's vivid Muckraking denouncement of the "embalmed beef trust" (1905) must be read alongside Professor C. B. Kuhlmann's dispassionate survey of the technical progress brought about in the meat-packing industry through the entrepreneurship of the so-called "Beef Barons," like Swift and Armour.

Pirates or pioneers? Can the student of history balance the piracy against the pioneering? How are historical judgements made? By balance-sheet? Can we mechanically check off against the name of each "Robber Baron" so many sins and so many innovations? Can sound judgments (historical or otherwise) be formulated in this fashion? Russell's attack consists mainly of one assertion after another, with little concrete evidence. It typifies one kind of "Muckraking" writing. Yet Russell does bring home with great force and clarity the wide reach of influence of the meat-packing leaders. Professor Kuhlmann's scholarly piece, on the other hand, describes the evolution of certain technical improvements which he attributes directly to Swift, Armour, and Morris. "New developments in packing," says Kuhlmann, "are associated with the rise of the captains of industry in this field." Does the evidence he offers really support this claim? Are the contributions made by the business leaders (if indeed they can be directly attributed to these leaders) especially significant or startling?

Obviously, the more technical the industry, the less easy it is to apply the label "Robber Baron" with a clear conscience. In the highly technical electronics field, masters like Edison and Westinghouse were scientists as well as businessmen. As the American economy moves beyond 1900 this combination of functions becomes much harder to maintain. How is the student of history to judge the inventor–businessman? Dr. H. C. Passer's skilled analysis of the career lines of Edison and Westinghouse in the new electrical industries throws much light on this question.

Passer takes us beyond the "Robber Baron" idea altogether, into a more sophisticated appreciation of the role of dynamic scientific leadership in the emergence of a whole new branch of the industrial economy. He emphasizes the scientific and technical difficulties that had to be overcome, and Edison and Westinghouse emerge, of course, as pioneers *par excellence*. How does this evidence affect our general judgment of the Robber Barons? Dr. Passer's information forces us to take more notice of technology; but can we use the field of electronics as a basis for broader generalizations about business leadership? The "a.c.-d.c. controversy," or Westinghouse's technique for conveying gas under high pressure, are a far cry from Jay Gould's stock-watering tricks. Is the electrical industry simply a special case? Anyone who concludes that it is must still remember Dr. Passer's strong argument that Edison was driven by commercial instincts, and that *because* his pioneering was "profit-oriented" it produced rapid application of new processes and contributed greatly to national economic growth. Edison's business instincts were as important as his scientific skills. Meanwhile, the Muckraker T. W. Lawson shows that old-fashioned "Robber Baron" activities were also to be found in the newer and more technical industries. Lawson gives a dramatic black-and-white tale of George Westinghouse's struggle with the powers of Wall Street, which throws into high relief the distinction between types of business activity — speculative and industrial.

With a larger and growing body of historical evidence now at hand, how have recent observers viewed the Robber Baron controversy? Some revisionist historians have countered the more serious indictments of late-nineteenth-century American business leaders with such arguments as the following. Financial ignorance was at least as large a cause of panics on the stock exchanges as deliberate stock manipulation. (Julius Grodinsky, for example, points out that Jay Gould operated in an era of general financial ignorance.) If the politicians were indeed corrupted by the businessmen, then they must have been corruptible; venality is the other side of bribery. If wages could have been higher and unions were solidly opposed, it is also true that American wages and living-standards were the highest in the world during the Gilded Age; this attracted the immigrants, and contract labor was only a tiny fraction of immigration as a whole. As for the consumer, whose fate H. D. Lloyd and others bemoaned, American consumer prices fell consistently over the whole period as a result of technical innovations and the emergence of mass, continuous-flow production methods. Competitive methods such as rebates (if not drawbacks) were nothing more in essence than quantity discounts, which were practiced widely in American industry and in some cases cancelled each other out. Competition was admittedly fierce; but it was not always so uneven. In the oil industry for example, as Allan Nevins has shown, the oil producers were as keen to subjugate the Cleveland refiners as Rockefeller and his refining colleagues were to take over the producers.

The strongest single answer to the charges against business leaders has been, as the readings by Grodinsky, Nevins, Meade, Kuhlmann, and Passer show, that they brought rapid economic growth. Through their technical skills, administrative genius, and financial acumen they are said to have rationalized American industries, unified them and integrated their processes vertically and horizontally; achieved great economies of scale; used countless byproducts previously wasted through ignorance and lack of efficient organization, capitalization and research. Further it has been said that they brought order and stability to vital sectors of economic life, eliminating needless and wasteful competition, abolishing dangerous price fluctuations, and ensuring steady supplies of raw materials and finished goods. As philanthropists in later life, some of them (notably Rockefeller and Carnegie) also served important welfare and educational functions.

This line of argument about the so-called Robber Barons is not fully accepted by all recent historians. Allen Solganick, for example, considers in turn each of several major propositions made in favor of the business leaders and rejects them all. For Solganick the activities of the Robber Barons took place against a backdrop of growing income inequality, increasing popular unrest with business, labor troubles, and increasing monopoly. The trust bosses did not lead the United States to unprecedented economic growth — in fact America's growth record in the Gilded Age, he argues, was not especially dramatic compared with rates achieved later by other nations. Moreover the industrial capitalists were not noteworthy for taking risks by introducing new technology. Above all, Solganick berates the revisionist (by which he means pro-business) scholars for refusing to face the facts, and for ignoring evidence which he regards as conclusive proof of the Robber Barons' guilt. The revisionists, according to this view, have not uncovered any new evidence but have merely reinterpreted old evidence.

In contrast to Professor Solganick's article, some other writers have emphasized, not the amassing of new historical evidence on the Robber Barons, but the need to create a meaningful theoretical framework — a general theory of business evolution and of the role of the business leader — within which to place existing evidence. Professor William Woodruff of the University of Melbourne made this point in an article on "History and the Businessmen" in the *Business History Review* of 1956. Armed with a workable scientific hypothesis, historians could go beyond the Robber Baron–captain of industry polarity altogether, neither praising the business leader nor condemning him, but seeking merely to understand him in his social–historical context. The selection by Alfred D. Chandler, Jr., does precisely this. Nowhere in it does Professor Chandler make any reference to the Robber Baron concept. He focusses attention on the administrative and technical problems of big business, the evolution of increasingly complex business structures in response to changing market conditions and industrial patterns. In his view entrepreneurship evolves by stages into a trained, professional function. His prose is neutral, his aim is descriptive analysis. For Chandler and the newer business historians, the Robber Baron controversy is simply an historical irrelevancy. The business leaders of the Gilded Age were neither Robbers nor Barons, but plain businessmen.

From Henry Demarest Lloyd to Alfred Chandler, Jr., the extended Robber Baron debate takes us from the days when economic history as a discipline was in its infancy — from the "literature of exposure" of the 1880's and 90's in which flamboyant, individualistic figures were painted with broad splashes of color by Muckraking journalists — to the sociologically inclined group studies of entrepreneurial leadership and the technical administrative histories being written today. But does the changing character of business history eliminate the problem of the Robber Barons? Does it help us to resolve the debate over whether they were pirates or pioneers? Or do the latest scholars, in seeking to avoid the oversimplifications involved in the pirate–pioneer dichotomy, only sidestep the issue? Professor Solganick does not sidestep; he takes a moral stand. Professor Chandler aims at scientific neutrality. In practice, however, since the bulk of past writing on the entrepreneurs has been heavily critical, even a neutral approach is bound to leave them in a more favorable historical light. Does the historical evidence justify this presentation? Or will the old Robber Baron image still prevail?

CONTENTS

I. THE CONTROVERSY STATED BY MEN OF THE DAY

HENRY DEMAREST LLOYD
> The Lords of Industry Destroy Free Enterprise   1

EDWARD ATKINSON
> But Don't Great Capitalists Spread the Wealth?   10

II. THE ROBBER BARONS — WHO WERE THEY?

ANDREW CARNEGIE
> Rags to Riches — The Poor Boy Makes Good   15

WILLIAM MILLER
> Men at the Top — A "WASP" Elite   18

III. THE ROBBER BARONS AS PIRATES

A. Railroads and Railroading

JAMES BRYCE
> The Railroad Kings — America's Greatest Men   27

MATTHEW JOSEPHSON
> Jay Gould — Classic Villain   30

JULIUS GRODINSKY
> Jay Gould — Capital Creator   38

B. Tricks of the Oil Trade: Rebates and Drawbacks

HENRY DEMAREST LLOYD
> The South Improvement Company — A "Fiendish Conspiracy"   47

ALLAN NEVINS
> The South Improvement Company — A Quest for Stability   57

C. The Price War in Sugar

COMMITTEE ON MANUFACTURES
    A Trust Is Formed   63

UNITED STATES INDUSTRIAL COMMISSION
    Sugar Refiners Struggle to Survive   67

GUSTAVUS MYERS
    They Plunder the Treasury   75

IV. THE ROBBER BARONS AS PIONEERS

EDWARD S. MEADE
    Carnegie Innovates   79

J. H. BRIDGE
    Carnegie Hesitates   83

CHARLES EDWARD RUSSELL
    The Beef Trust Grows Fat   86

CHARLES B. KUHLMANN
    The Beef Barons Revolutionize the Food Industry   89

HAROLD C. PASSER
    The Inventor–Businessmen: Westinghouse and Edison   93

THOMAS W. LAWSON
    Pioneers and Speculators — Westinghouse versus "the
        System"   102

V. THE CONTROVERSY RESTATED BY RECENT OBSERVERS

ALLEN SOLGANICK
    Pirates   106

ALFRED D. CHANDLER, JR.
    Neither Robbers nor Barons, but Businessmen   114

Suggestions for Additional Reading   125

I. THE CONTROVERSY STATED BY MEN OF THE DAY

Henry Demarest Lloyd: THE LORDS OF INDUSTRY DESTROY FREE ENTERPRISE

A well-to-do journalist for many years associated with the Chicago Tribune, Henry Demarest Lloyd (1847–1903) was the most influential contemporary critic of the Robber Barons. This first of two selections from his work, an article of 1884, gives the standard reform case against monopolists — that they destroy free competition and fix consumer prices. But Lloyd was no dogmatic adherent of "free competition." In later life he went further than some of his Progressive colleagues towards government intervention and regulated competition. Shortly before his death he considered becoming a Socialist. Lloyd's writing is heavily illustrated with examples. Historians have sharply disagreed over the accuracy of some of his evidence.

ADAM SMITH said in 1776: "People of the same trade hardly meet together even for merriment and diversion but the conversation ends in a conspiracy against the public, or in some contrivance to raise prices." The expansive ferment of the New Industry, coming with the new science, the new land, and the new liberties of our era, broke up these "conspiracies," and for a century we have heard nothing of them; but the race to overrun is being succeeded by the struggle to divide, and combinations are reappearing on all sides. This any one may see from the reports of the proceedings of the conventions and meetings of innumerable associations of manufacturers and dealers and even producers, which are being held almost constantly. They all do something to raise prices, or hold them up, and they wind up with banquets for which we pay.

Four years ago the Chicago Lumbermen's Exchange adopted a resolution declaring it to be "dishonorable" for any dealer to make lower prices than those published by it for the control of prices in one of the greatest lumber markets of the world. Monthly reports are required by this Exchange from dealers, so that accurate accounts may be kept of stock on hand in order to regulate prices. The price lists of the Exchange are revised and made "honest" at monthly banquets. . . .

. . . The lumber market of the Pacific coast is ruled by the California Lumber Exchange, and that is controlled by a few powerful firms. The prices of red-wood are fixed by the Redwood Manufacturers' Association, and those of pine by the Pine Manufacturers' Association. During the past year the retail dealers of San Francisco have had to sign contracts with these associations, binding themselves to buy only from members of the associa-

From Henry Demarest Lloyd, "Lords of Industry," *The North American Review*, Vol. CCCXXXI (June, 1884), abridged.

tions, to buy and sell only at prices fixed by them, to give time and discount only according to rule, and keep accounts so that every item will be clear to the inspectors hired by the associations to look after the retailers. Finally, the retailer binds himself, if he is "found guilty" of committing any of the forbidden sins, to pay a fine which may amount to one thousand dollars, to be divided among the faithful. The literature of business can show no more remarkable productions than the printed forms of these contracts. This system is in imitation of the "special contracts" with shippers which have been put in force by the Central Pacific Railroad.

Western ranch-men complain that the competition of buyers is disappearing. They declare that there exist at the Chicago stock-yards combinations of buyers who, by their ability to make large purchases and their agreement to offer but one price, get cattle at their own figures. One member of the "ring" does the buying to-day; another to-morrow, and so on. . . .

Last July Messrs. Vanderbilt, Sloan, and one or two others out of several hundred owners of coal lands and coal railroads, met in the pleasant shadows of Saratoga to make "a binding arrangement for the control of the coal trade." "Binding arrangement" the sensitive coal presidents say they prefer to the word "combination." The gratuitous warmth of summer suggested to these men the need the public would have of artificial heat, at artificial prices, the coming winter. It was agreed to fix prices, and to prevent the production of too much of the raw material of warmth, by suspensions of mining. In anticipation of the arrival of the cold wave from Manitoba, a cold wave was sent out all over the United States, from their parlors in New York, in

an order for half-time work by the miners during the first three months of this year, and for an increase of prices. These are the means this combination uses to keep down wages — the price of men, and keep up the price of coal — the wages of capital. Prices of coal in the West are fixed by the Western Anthracite Coal Association, controlled entirely by the large railroads and mine-owners of Pennsylvania. This association regulates the price west of Buffalo and Pittsburgh and in Canada. Our annual consumption of anthracite is now between 31,000,000 and 32,000,000 tons. The West takes between 5,000,000 and 6,000,000 tons. The companies which compose the combination mine, transport, and sell their own coal. They are obliterating other mine-owners and the retailer. The Chicago and New York dealer has almost nothing to say about what he shall pay or what he shall charge, or what his profits shall be. The great companies do not let the little men make too much. Year by year the coal retailers are sinking into the status of mere agents of the combination, with as little freedom as the consumer.

There was an investigation of the coal combination by the Pennsylvania legislature in 1871, the testimony taken in which showed, as summarized in "The Nation," then the leading anti-monopoly paper in the United States, that when, after a thirty-days' strike by the men, a number of private coal-mine owners acceded to their terms and wished to re-open their mines and send coal again to market, the railroads, by which alone they could get to market, raised their freights, as their men were still on strike, to three times the previous figures. These great corporations had determined not to yield to their men, and as they were mine-owners and coal-sellers as well as carriers, they refused to take coal for their competitors.

Manipulation
of economy,
not free + open

The latter, if they could have got transportation, would have given their own men employment and supplied the people of the country with coal. This would have compelled the great companies either to make terms with their workmen, or to let these other mine-owners take the trade. Instead of doing so, they used their power over the only available means of transportation to dictate the terms upon which every other employer should deal with his men, by preventing him from sending his products to market so long as he granted his men better terms than those laid down by the company. The result was that the price of coal was doubled, rising to $12 a ton; the resumption by the private mine-owners was stopped; and they, the workmen and the consumer, were all delivered over to the tender mercies of the six great companies. . . .

Combination is busy in those soft-coal districts, whose production is so large that it must be sent to competitive markets. A pool has just been formed covering the annual product of 6,000,000 tons of the mines of Ohio. Indiana and Illinois are to be brought in, and it is planned to extend it to all the bituminous coal districts that compete with each other. The appearance of Mr. Vanderbilt, last December, in the Clearfield district of Pennsylvania, at the head of a company capitalized for $5,000,000, was the first entry of a metropolitan mind into this field. Mr. Vanderbilt's rôle is to be that of producer, carrier, dealer, and consumer, all in one. Until he came, the district was occupied by a number of small companies and small operators, as used to be the case in the anthracite field in the old days. But the man who works himself, with his sons, in a small mine, cutting perhaps from twenty to forty tons a day, cannot expect to survive the approach of the Manhattan capitalist. The small Clearfield producers, looking at the fate of their kind in the anthracite country, greeted Mr. Vanderbilt's arrival with the question, "What is to become of us?" "If the small operator," said one of the great man's lieutenants, "goes to the wall, that is his misfortune, not our fault." In March last the prominent Clearfield companies gave notice that wages must be reduced on the 1st of April, and immediately thereafter a union of their employés resolved that if the reduction, which they declared to be "without reason," was made they would strike. . . .

There has been since 1872 a national combination of the manufacturers of the stoves, into which the combination coal must be put; and its effect, the founder said, in his speech at the annual banquet in Cleveland, last February, had been to change the balance from the wrong to the right side of the ledger. Until lately, at least, combination matches lighted the fire of combination coal in these combination stoves, and it is combination oil which the cook, contrary to orders, puts on the fires to make them burn faster. The combination of match manufacturers was perfected by the experience of sixteen years of fusions, till lately it shared with the coal combination the pleasure of advancing the price of fire by proclamation on the approach of winter. It is now at war with the new companies which have gone into the manufacture since the repeal of the internal revenue tax. These it is attempting to conquer by underselling them, tactics which have hitherto never failed. The Government of the United States, before which all men are equal, helped this combination to kill off its competitors, shielding it from foreign competition by a tax of thirty-five per cent. on the importation of matches from abroad, and shielding it from domestic competition, by administering the internal revenue tax so as to make its small competitors pay ten per cent. more tax. This drove them into bankruptcy, or combination with the ring, at the rate of one or two every month. The railroads, like the Government, helped to transfer this business from the many to a few, by carrying the combination's matches at lower rates than were given to its little competitors.

When the house-maid strikes a combination match on the wall-paper, she leaves a mark on an article the manufacture, sale, and price of which are rigidly regulated by the American Wall Paper Manufacturers' Association. A recent writer has described this oath-bound combination which has established a wallpaper monarchy in the United States. When the cook takes the paper from off the express package, the hardware, the dry-goods, the groceries, the candy, the ham, which have been sent home, she is still handling an article the price of which is fixed by private enactments. The Western Wrapping-paper Association, ever since 1880, has, with more or less success, been struggling to keep down the deluge of too much wrapping-paper, and to fix the prices of all kinds, from the paper under the carpet to that which is used in roofing. It recently failed, but was at once reorganized on a firmer footing than before, and its mills are now allowed to turn out but one-half as much as they could produce. Besides this, the wood pulp and straw paper industries have been amalgamated. The American Paper Association aims to control the prices and production of paper for newspapers and books, and for writing. The dealers in old rags and old paper formed an association in Cleveland three years ago to deal with the "old-rag" problem of how to cut down the enormous profits the women of our country are making out of the contents of their rag-bags. In January, 1883, the trade met again at Rochester, formed two "national" associations, and solemnly agreed upon the prices to be paid for mixed rags "that we gather from house to house," and for brown paper and rag carpet. "No change of price for rags or paper," runs the decree of the old-rag barons, "is to be made without consultation of every member of the executive committee." The Western Wooden Ware Association discovered, last December, that there were too many pails, tubs, and bowls, and ordered its members to manufacture but one-fifth of their capacity. In February it gave them permission to increase this to one-half. The Western Cracker Bakers' Association met in Chicago in February to consider, among other things, "the reprehensible system of cutting prices." They first had a banquet. After their "merriment and diversion" the revelers, true to Adam Smith's description, turned to consider "some contrivance to raise prices." "The price lists were perfected," said the newspaper report, and then they adjourned.

The men who make our shrouds and coffins have formed a close corporation known as the National Burial Case Association, and held their national convention in Chicago last year. Their action to keep up prices and keep down the number of coffins was secret, lest mortality should be discouraged. The largest manufacturers of quinine in the world are the Boehringers of Milan, Mannheim, and Paris. The next largest are Powers and Weightman of Philadelphia. The latter have just leased the Boehringer factory in Mannheim. New York druggists say that these two could force up the price of quinine very high by combination, but do not believe they will do so.

A pool of the seventeen leading quinine manufacturers of the world was formed last July. It included the manufacturers of America, Great Britain, and the continent of Europe. It advanced prices for a time twenty cents an ounce, but went to pieces at the beginning of 1884. The manufacturers of patent medicines organized in 1883, and the wholesale and retail druggists have followed with organizations to prevent the sale of these nostrums at cut prices, or by any persons who were not regular druggists. A "drug war" has broken out and threatens to rage over the entire Union. The combination of the wholesale druggists and that of the manufacturers have mutually agreed to divide the United States into districts, each of which shall be under a superintendent, who is to watch the druggists and report all those cutting prices, who are thereupon to be boycotted.

Every one knows about the thirty-million-dollar steel combination, which has not kept the price of rails from declining from $166 a ton in 1867 to $32 a ton in 1884, but during this decline has kept the price of rails — that is, the price of transportation, that is, the price of everything, higher in this country than anywhere else. Chairman Morrison of the Committee of Ways and Means is a witness to the fact that the chimneys of the Vulcan Mill at St. Louis stood smokeless for years, and meanwhile its owners received a subsidy reported at $400,000 a year from the other mills of the combination for not making rails, with, however, no payment to its men for not working. The steel-rail makers of England, France, Belgium, and Germany are negotiating for an international combination to keep up prices. The "Age of Steel" startled the country last January by the statement that a monster pool was to be formed of all our pig-iron manufacturers. The country was to be divided into six districts. As many furnaces were to be put out of blast as were necessary to prevent us from having too much iron, and these idle furnaces were to share, like the Vulcan Steel Mill, the profits of those that ran. This has not yet proved to be history, but it may turn out to have been prophecy.

There are too many nails for the nail-makers, though no such complaint has been heard from the house-builders. There is a nail association, which at the beginning of the year advanced prices ten cents a keg. Last November it ordered a suspension of the nail machines for five weeks, to the great distress of eight thousand workmen, who are also machines — self-feeders. "We hope," said the nail-men, according to a Pittsburgh dispatch of December 29, 1882, "to show consumers that we can not only control production, but that we can do so unanimously, and at the very time when nails are the least wanted." On April 9th, of this year, the nail manufacturers of the West met again at Pittsburgh, and adopted the most modern form of pool, with managers having full powers to regulate prices and restrict production. "An early advance of prices may be expected," we are told. Every mill in the West is in the pool. Nail-buyers are not allowed to converse with nail-makers. All business must be done through the Board of Control.

There is too much barbed wire for the wire manufacturers, though not for the farmers, and a pool, under the "entire control" of eleven directors, has, within a few weeks, been formed, in which are enrolled all of the chief manufacturers. Its members met in March in St. Louis, and advanced prices. They met again in Chicago, April 4th, and advanced prices

10 per cent., and adjourned to meet in thirty days for the purpose of making another advance. This combination cuts off competition at both ends. It confederates the makers, so that they shall not sell in competition with each other, and it buys all its raw material through one purchasing agent, so that its members do not buy in competition. The Western Pig Iron Association regard "the cutting of prices as the bane of business," and do what they can to stop it. Thirteen concerns making wrought-iron pipes in this country met in December last to unite under the very appropriate name of the Empire Iron Company. Each was to deposit $20,000 as security that he would adhere to rules to prevent the calamity of too much iron pipe. One feature of the pool was that it proposed to keep men on guard at each mill, to keep account of the pipe made and shipped; and these superintendents were to be moved around from one mill to another at least once every eight weeks. April 1, 1882, when the rest of us were lost in the reckless gayety of All Fools' Day, forty-one tack manufacturers found out that there were too many tacks, and formed the "Central Manufacturing Company of Boston," with $3,000,000 capital. The tackmills in the combination run about three days in the week. When this combination, a few weeks ago, silenced a Pittsburgh rival by buying him out, they did not remove the machinery. The dead chimneys and idle machines will discourage new men from starting another factory, or can be run to ruin them if they are not to be discouraged in any other way. The first-fruits of the tack-pool were an increase of prices to twice what they had been.

One of the objections raised thousands of years ago in Greece, against the union of people of the same trade, was that their meetings degenerated into political conspiracies, and Trajan, for the same reason, refused to accede to the request of Pliny that he might enroll a fire company out of the workmen of Nicomedia. No precautions, said the shrewd emperor, can prevent such associations from becoming dangerous conspiracies. The whisky distillers' pool is a combination of all the distillers north of the Ohio River from Pittsburgh to the Pacific Ocean. It regulates production, export, and prices. Its success at Washington, in securing legislation several years ago granting whisky makers the privilege, given to no other tax-payer, of a postponement of the time for payment of taxes, is a significant reminder of Trajan's saying. The demand for whisky so far falls short of the capacity of the pool to produce, that a large number of distilleries are kept idle, drawing pensions from the combination, in some cases as high as $500 a day. The Brewers and Maltsters' Association of New York fixes the prices of beer by combination, and claims to control 35,000 votes. It takes to itself the credit of the defeat, last year, of Mr. Maynard, candidate for Secretary of State of New York. At the last session of the association the suggestion was made by one of the speakers, that if the brewers would see that the foreigners in their employ took out naturalization papers, they would, no doubt, "cast their votes properly."

The publishers of school books do not like competition — that is, what they call "dishonest competition." Nineteen of the leading firms of the country have formed a combination, by which they are bound to obey the orders of an executive committee as to prices and other matters. This, says the "Age of Steel," will be cheerful news to the heads of families, who already have enough half-worn school books in the house to have stocked a whole township forty years ago. A heavy penalty is imposed upon any publisher who supplants the books of another house in the pool by reducing prices or otherwise. The successful man has to hand over to the unsuccessful one the value of the book for three years. The Ohio Senate recently discussed means for overcoming this combination and securing competition in the supply of school books to the State as of old.

The competition of the fire insurance companies, which broke out in 1875, upon the collapse of their pool, cost them in New York city alone $17,500,000 in seven years, and in 1882 they made a new combination which covered the whole country, and is, in point of wealth and cohesiveness, one of the most powerful and most successful in the country. The combination of makers of stamped tinware, formed in 1882, expelled members who sold at lower than the fixed rates, and refused to allow any one in the pool to sell to the offenders. The situation was so uncomfortable, that the expelled deliberated whether to prosecute the association for conspiracy or to pay the penalty and go back into the fold; they chose to do the latter. . . .

Such are some of the pools into which our industry is eddying. They come and go, but more come than go, and those that stay grow. All are "voluntary," of course, but if the milk farmer of Orange county, the iron molder of Troy, the lumber dealer of San Francisco, the Lackawanna Railroad, or any other individual or corporate producer, show any backwardness about accepting the invitation to join "the pool," they are whipped in with all the competitive weapons at command, from assault and battery to boycotting and conspiracy. The private wars that are ravaging our world of trade give small men their choice between extermi-

nation and vassalage. Combine or die! The little coke burner of Connellsville works or stops work, the coal dealer of Chicago raises his prices or lowers them, the type-setter takes up his stick or lays it down, as the master of the pool directs. Competitors swear themselves on the Bible into accomplices, and free and equal citizens abandon their business privacy to pool commissioners vested with absolute power, but subject to human frailties. Commerce is learning the delights of universal suffrage, and in scores of trades supply and demand are adjusted by a majority vote. In a society which has the wherewithal to cover, fatten and cheer every one, Lords of Industry are acquiring the power to pool the profits of scarcity and to decree famine. They cannot stop the brook that runs the mill, but they can chain the wheel; they cannot hide the coal mine, but they can close the shaft three days every week. To keep up gold-digging rates of dividends, they declare war against plenty. On all that keeps him alive the workman must pay them their prices, while they lock him out of the mill in which alone his labor can be made to fetch the price of life. Only society can compel a social use of its resources; the man is for himself.

On the theory of "too much of everything" our industries, from railroads to workingmen, are being organized to prevent milk, nails, lumber, freights, labor, soothing syrup, and all these other things, from becoming too cheap. The majority have never yet been able to buy enough of anything. The minority have too much of everything to sell. Seeds of social trouble germinate fast in such conditions. Society is letting these combinations become institutions without compelling them to adjust their charges to the cost of production, which used to be the universal rule of price. Our laws and commissions to regulate the railroads are but toddling steps in a path in which we need to walk like men. The change from competition to combination is nothing less than one of those revolutions which march through history with giant strides. It is not likely that this revolution will go backward. Nothing goes backward in this country except reform. When Stephenson said of railroads that where combination was possible competition was impossible, he was unconsciously declaring the law of all industry.

Man, the only animal which forgets, has already in a century or two forgotten that the freedom, the independence of his group, of the state and even of the family, which he has enjoyed for a brief interval, have been unknown in most of the history of our race, and in all the history of most races. The livery companies of London, with their gloomy guildhalls, their wealth, their gluttony and wine-bibbing, their wretched Irish estates, exist to-day vain reminders to us of a time when the entire industry of Europe was regimented into organizations, voluntary at first, afterward adopted by the law, which did what our pools of railroads, laborers, manufacturers, and others are trying to do. Not only prices but manners were pooled. "The notion," says Cliffe Leslie, "that every man had a right to settle where he liked, to carry on any occupation he thought fit, and in whatever manner he chose, to demand the highest price he could get, or on the contrary to offer lower terms than any one else, to make the largest profit possible, and to compete with other traders without restraint, was absolutely contrary to the spirit of the ages that preceded ours." This system existed for centuries. It is so unlike our own that the contemplation of it may well shake us out of our

conceit that the transitions, displacements, changes, upheavals, struggles, exterminations — from Indians to sewing women — of the last two hundred and fifty years were the normal condition of the race.

Those were not exceptional times. Our day of free competition and free contract has been the exceptional era in history. Explorer, pioneer, protestant, reformer, captain of industry could not move in the harness of the guild brother, the vassal, the monk, and were allowed to throw away mediæval uniforms. But now "the individual withers; the world is more and more." Society having let the individual overrun the new worlds to be conquered, is reëstablishing its lines of communication with him. Literary theorists still repeat the cant of individualism in law, politics, and morals; but the world of affairs is gladly accepting, in lieu of the liberty of each to do as he will with his own, all it can get of the liberty given by laws that let no one do as he might with his own. The dream of the French Revolution, that man was good enough to be emancipated from the bonds of association and government by the simple proclamation of Liberty, Fraternity and Equality, was but the frenzied expression of what was called Freedom of Self-interest in a quieter but not less bloody revolution, if the mortality of the factories, the mines, and the tenements be charged to its account. A rope cannot be made of sand; a society cannot be made of competitive units.

We have given competition its own way, and have found that we are not good enough or wise enough to be trusted with this power of ruining ourselves in the attempt to ruin others. Free competition could be let run only in a community where every one had learned to say and act "I am the state." We have had an era of material inventions. We now need a renaissance of moral inventions, contrivances to tap the vast currents of moral magnetism flowing uncaught over the face of society. Morals and values rise and fall together. If our combinations have no morals, they can have no values. If the tendency to combination is irresistible, control of it is imperative. Monopoly and anti-monopoly, odious as these words have become to the literary ear, represent the two great tendencies of our time: monopoly, the tendency to combination; anti-monopoly, the demand for social control of it. As the man is bent toward business or patriotism, he will negotiate combinations or agitate for laws to regulate them. The first is capitalistic, the second is social. The first, industrial; the second, moral. The first promotes wealth; the second, citizenship. These combinations are not to be waved away as fresh pictures of folly or total depravity. There is something in them deeper than that. The Aryan has proved by the experience of thousands of years that he can travel. "But travel," Emerson says, "is the fool's paradise." We must now prove that we can stay at home, and stand it as well as the Chinese have done. Future Puritans cannot emigrate from Southampton to Plymouth Rock. They can only sail from righteousness to righteousness. Our young men can no longer go west; they must go up or down. Not new land, but new virtue must be the outlet for the future. Our halt at the shores of the Pacific is a much more serious affair than that which brought our ancestors to a pause before the barriers of the Atlantic, and compelled them to practice living together for a few hundred years. We cannot hereafter, as in the past, recover freedom by going to the prairies; we must find it in the society of the good. In the presence of great combinations, in all departments of life, the moralist and patriot have work to do of a significance never before approached during the itinerant phases of our civilization. It may be that the coming age of combination will issue in a nobler and fuller liberty for the individual than has yet been seen, but that consummation will be possible, not in a day of competitive trade, but in one of competitive morals.

Edward Atkinson: BUT DON'T GREAT CAPITALISTS SPREAD THE WEALTH?

Edward Atkinson (1827–1905) could not present a greater contrast to Lloyd. Devoted to the life of business, he was successful for many years in cotton manufacturing before moving over into fire insurance in 1878. An enthusiastic pamphleteer, this New England businessman became a major spokesman for tariff reform, anti-imperialism, and the "New South." (He invented among other devices an automatic fire-door, and he encouraged the spread of automatic fire-sprinklers). In this lively address of 1886, Atkinson argues that the capitalist is not a mere profiteer but a creative, pioneering entrepreneur — to whom the worker and the general public are indebted for wages and cheaper products. His argument is still heard today.

ANOTHER mistake which is constantly made is that the capitalist is getting a very big share of the product of almost every thing. This is not so, especially in the arts in which capital is most freely used.

Now, what are the facts? If a man could build a cotton-mill to-day, at the prices of materials and machinery, to make heavy sheetings, spending one million dollars on it, he would make in that factory goods worth about one and one-quarter million dollars every year, at six cents a yard. If he could get one-third to one-quarter of a cent a yard, he could keep up his factory and earn six per cent on his investment.

What would become of the other five and three-quarters?

It would be spent for materials, for labor, and for the salary of a superintendent competent to put the materials and the labor together, unless the owner were his own boss.

Some of you know what it is to work in a mill under an incompetent manager or an incompetent owner, who cannot put the materials and the labor together in a proper way.

When such a fellow as that takes hold, the workman loses his wages, and the owner loses his profit and generally loses his mill.

The cheapest man is the one who *knows how to do it,* no matter what his price is. Just as the cheapest workman is the best workman, no matter what *his* price is. . . .

About one-fifth of all the capital in the United States, of every name and nature, is to-day invested in railroads. There is more fuss made about the big fortunes of the railroad capitalists than of any other; but there are only one or two of them who have stolen their share or cheated other people out of it. There is no defence for such men.

But there are other men who have not cheated anybody, — men of the most honorable character, who build railroads, operate them honestly and fairly, and who have made big fortunes out of them. How did they do it?

Some of you live out at Olneyville very likely, or about that distance away from Providence. If an expressman owning a car would carry a barrel of flour for you, from a store in Providence out to your

From Edward Atkinson, *Addresses Upon the Labor Question* (Boston, 1886), pp. 13–26, abridged.

house, you would give him the empty barrel for his profit, wouldn't you, provided you could not do any better? and you would feel very well satisfied with the bargain.

Very well. Vanderbilt ran a cart from Chicago to Providence, with a steam-engine instead of a horse, over the Lake Shore and New York Central railroads. He carted, or some other man did, who ran another railroad alongside of his, all the flour that you ate last year, from Chicago to Providence, about one thousand miles, for sixty-eight cents a barrel, or less; very often less.

What profit did he make? Fourteen cents a barrel; no more; sometimes less. Not so much as the value of the empty barrel.

What if he did make two hundred millions of dollars or more by the job, he and his father working together twenty-five or thirty years? Wasn't he a cheap man for you to employ as a teamster? Didn't he cart flour cheaply enough? Do you grudge him the fourteen cents? . . .

In 1865 the New York Central, Vanderbilt line, charged three dollars forty-five cents for moving a barrel of flour one thousand miles. Last year they charged sixty-eight cents, sometimes less.

The difference between these two prices on the flour consumed by the people of the United States last year was one hundred thirty-eight million, five hundred thousand dollars. Your share of the saving, each of you (for you each need one barrel of flour per year, for each adult member of your family), was two dollars seventy-seven cents a barrel. Vanderbilt made his two hundred million dollars by cheapening the cost of carrying the flour, and saving each of us two dollars seventy-seven cents, last year, on our flour. . . .

Bread is the staff of life. And, although

man does not live by bread alone, we must each have one barrel of flour a year. Now, one man, working one year (or what is the same thing, three men each working one hundred days in the season) can raise wheat enough in Dakota to supply one thousand men with flour for one year.

Of what use would this wheat be to us, if we could not get it? How could we get it from a place two thousand miles away, except by way of a railroad? Some people say labor does all the work, and ought therefore to have all the product. True: let labor go to Dakota, and bring the flour two thousand miles to Providence on a wheelbarrow, and it may have all the profit. I prefer to hire a capitalist to bring my barrel.

There is a big strike on what is called the "Gould" system of railroads. It is, or was, alleged that the strike will extend until it covers the whole railroad system between the East and West.

Well, suppose this should happen. Who will be struck the hardest, and who will pay the costs? Capitalists who own the railroads? Not a bit of it. *You will.* The wages of the men who are employed upon the railroads are never paid out of the capital invested in them. It would not be possible. They would eat up the railroads, if they ate up the capital. Then what? The wages of the men who operate the railroads are paid out of the current receipts for moving food and fuel, timber and dry goods, which you use or eat. You pay them. How many of railroad men are there? About five men to a mile, — 625,000 in the whole United States.

There are now twenty million men and women at work in the United States; and those who work for wages, earn small salaries, or run small farms by hard labor, count nearly nineteen million out of the twenty million, and consume nineteen-twentieths of all that is produced or moved over all the railroads.

This body of the railroad men is one of the largest single divisions, and they are among the best paid. You pay them, each one your share.

Last year the New York Central Railroad earned its part of a profit of fourteen cents a barrel, for moving a barrel of flour a thousand miles. In their part of the work, this corporation employed 15,309 men and boys, and I suppose a few women as clerks. They paid them an average of $544.60 a year each for their work. That is to say, you paid your share to the railroad, and the railroad paid the men at this rate. This railroad business is the most wonderful thing in the world. Some of you think labor does all the work, and ought to have all the pay; and some of these shallow fellows, tonguey chaps, get up and talk about the tyranny of capital, and say that these great corporations rule the country. Well, perhaps they do. I will give you some figures. Last year the railroads of the United States moved a little over four hundred million tons an average distance of a hundred and ten miles. You can't comprehend such big figures, unless you are used to them. What did they move? What was all the fuss about? Why couldn't they let it alone? Why couldn't they let labor do all the work, and take all the pay?

They moved cotton and corn, wool and mutton, beef and pork, timber and coal, iron and groceries, what for? Only that you and I might have breakfast, dinner, and supper, a roof over our heads, some clothes to wear, some fuel to burn, and some tools to work with. What else? Well, just for that, over seven tons were moved a hundred and ten miles for every one of us, and for every one of our fami-

lies. As much for you as for me. Just as much for Terry Gallagher as for Cornelius Vanderbilt, — hardly any difference.

Think of it a minute — seven tons; seventy barrels of flour, or twenty-eight bales of cotton, or a hundred cases of sixteen-ounce cassimere, or fourteen big casks of sugar. Think of any other lot of food or dry goods, and how much work it would be to move each lot a hundred and ten miles, just to give each of us and each of our children breakfast, dinner, and supper, clothes, fuel, and shelter. What will you take to do the job, and how long will it take you? Labor does all the work, and ought to have all the pay — does it? Bid for it, then — who will do it at a dollar and twenty-five cents a ton? eight dollars and seventy-five cents for the job? That is what the great railway corporations got for it — no more. Shall I say nine dollars? Who bids ten dollars? Going, going, gone to the railroad every time; because the railroad saves you just so much work every year, as it would take to move that seven tons apiece a hundred and ten miles. If they didn't do this, how would you live, and where would you live? Do you grudge the New York Central its profit of fourteen cents a barrel for moving your barrel of flour a thousand miles? . . .

I tell you, my friends, you must get the bottom facts; don't let shysters throw dust in your eyes; it's devil's dust, poor shoddy, it won't wash. . . .

Suppose all these railroad-men strike, and get all the profit, out of which the interest on the debts and the dividends on the stock are paid, the corporation would then be unable to earn fourteen cents a barrel for moving a barrel of flour a thousand miles.

That would put the road into bankruptcy. Who would then take it up and run it? Of course this won't happen. But suppose the men strike on all the railroads, and the price of freight is put up. Who pays it? You pay it on every barrel of flour, ever ton of coal, every pound of beef which you use, or every yard of cloth which you make.

Suppose *you* strike back when there is no profit on cotton manufacturing or on woollen manufacturing. What happens then? Either the price of the goods must be put up, or the mill must stop. Who pays for that? The capitalist who owns the mill? Not a bit of it. He waits.

The men who run the railroads, the carpenters, masons, mechanics all over the country, pay for it in a higher price for goods.

Now, suppose we all strike. The measure of enough is a little more. I should like to strike, and get a little more. You would like to strike, and get a little more. The next man would like to strike, and get a little more. And when we have all struck, and all have got a little more, what have we accomplished and where are we?

For the time being we have had an interruption of business, a decrease of product, a temporary scarcity; and then the same kind of a distribution goes on — only at high prices, as it went on before at low prices. In the meantime, middlemen who happened to have a big stock of goods when the strike began will take the rise in price, and the rest of us will pay it.

What else can you make of it? None of us work for money, although we think we do. We work for what we can buy with our money. The important point is, that there should be the biggest product for the least amount of work. Large product, low prices, high wages, — that is what we all want.

Small rates of profit on capital come from big production, hard work for the capitalist (and perhaps he will get rich), but easier work for the laborer, lower prices, and higher wages . . .

Here is a man — well, we will take the late A. T. Stewart as an example. He set up a big shop, and everybody went to it to buy something, and Stewart made a big fortune, which is rapidly disappearing. How did he do it? Exactly in the way in which Vanderbilt ran a railroad. He hired the best men, distributed the goods at the lowest prices, at a small profit on each sale, but he made a big fortune out of very large sales.

Why did everybody go to his shop? In order to help make Stewart's fortune? Not a bit of it. Each one went there because he benefited himself, or thought he did, which is the same thing. He got the best goods for cash, at the lowest price.

If you could only find out a way to establish a big public market here in Providence, and systemize the distribution of food, meat, vegetables, or fruit, in the way in which Stewart organized and distributed dry goods, every man of you could save ten or fifteen, and perhaps twenty to twenty-five, per cent on the price that you now pay for a comparatively poor supply of the same food.

If you can't get the market in any other way, better hire an A. T. Stewart to do it, if you can find one.

The biggest problem waiting to be solved is how to distribute meat, fish, bread, beans, potatoes, and milk, etc., at the lowest cost.

There is a man named Samuel Howe in New York, who has a large capital, with which he has built a big bakery. He sells the best bread over the counter to any one who will come and carry it away, at three cents a pound. I cannot find any bread in Boston so good at five cents a pound.

It costs more to distribute bakers' bread after it is finished, and taken out of the oven, than it does to raise the wheat, or to grind it, or to move it fifteen hundred miles, or to bake it. All these elements of cost could be covered here in Providence with a profit, to the capitalist who works on a large scale, at three cents a pound. I venture to say, that, if you weigh the loaves of bread that you buy, you will find that you pay from five to eight cents a pound.

What are you going to do about it? Strike? or pass a law regulating the baking of bread, which will put up the price instead of putting it down?

Each man serves the other; and every man is a working man, except the drones: they are few in number, — relatively unimportant.

The capitalist does the largest service, and gets the best price per man at the smallest rate for each service.

The skilled workman comes next, and gets a good price because he does good work.

The common laborer does the least, and gets the least for it.

What are you going to do about it? Put the common laborer on top? . . .

In all honest work, the dollar of the man's earnings, whether measured at five hundred dollars a year, or five hundred thousand dollars, is the measure of the service which he has rendered, and for which he is paid. And it is because no man can live for himself alone, that no man can make profitable use of his capital without giving employment to some other man by such use. Capital is used in the service of labor, just as truly as labor is employed in the service of capital.

There is no Devil to take the hindmost, except the Devil has a fair claim upon him; and that is the hindmost man's own lookout, rather than yours or mine. We will do all we can to help him; but, after all, no other man can help a man who cannot help himself.

There is always plenty of room on the front seats in every profession, every trade, every art, every industry. There are men in this audience who will fill some of those seats, but they won't be boosted into them from behind; they will get there by using their own brains and their own hands. Do they keep other men out of those seats, or do they hold other men down in order to get them?

Did Vanderbilt keep any of you down, by saving you two dollars and seventy-five cents on a barrel of flour, while he was making fourteen cents?

II. THE ROBBER BARONS—
WHO WERE THEY?

Andrew Carnegie: RAGS TO RICHES — THE POOR BOY
MAKES GOOD

The classic American story of the poor boy who made good is surely that of Andrew Carnegie (1835–1919), who rose from the lowly position of bobbin-boy in a cotton textile mill in Allegheny, Pa., with earnings of $1.20 a week, to that of multimillionaire of the American steel industry. He eventually became a public philanthropist whose gifts totalled an estimated $350,000,000 and included 2,800 libraries, Carnegie Hall (1891), the Carnegie Institution of Washington (1902), the Carnegie Foundation for the Advancement of Teaching (1906), the Carnegie Endowment for International Peace (1910), the Carnegie Corporation of New York (1911), and the Carnegie Institute of Technology (1912). Carnegie philosophized a good deal about his amazing rise, and was an articulate and prolific writer of articles and books, of which perhaps the most remembered is his The Gospel of Wealth, *which first appeared as an article in the* North American Review *in June, 1889. Carnegie did not believe in inheritance, and emphasized the duty of the wealthy to spend their riches on public benefactions. In the selection from his* Autobiography *given below, Carnegie tells a simple story simply and well. He emigrated to the United States, with his family who were in near-poverty, in 1848 and left behind him a Scottish childhood background of radical politics, radical religion, and material insecurity. His first impressions of America did not seem promising; but the reading ends on a characteristic Carnegie note.*

TO begin, then, I was born in Dunfermline, in the attic of the small one-story house, corner of Moodie Street and Priory Lane, on the 25th of November, 1835, and, as the saying is, "of poor but honest parents, of good kith and kin." Dunfermline had long been noted as the center of the damask trade in Scotland. My father, William Carnegie, was a damask weaver, the son of Andrew Carnegie after whom I was named. . . .

As my father succeeded in the weaving business we removed from Moodie Street to a much more commodious house in Reid's Park. My father's four or five looms occupied the lower story; we resided in the upper, which was reached, after a fashion common in the older Scottish houses, by outside stairs from the pavement. . . .

The change from hand-loom to steam-loom weaving was disastrous to our family. My father did not recognize the impending revolution, and was struggling under the old system. His looms sank greatly in value, and it became necessary for that power which never failed in any emergency — my mother — to step forward and endeavor to repair the family fortune. She opened a small shop in Moodie Street and contributed to the revenues which, though slender, nevertheless at that time sufficed to keep us in comfort and "respectable."

I remember that shortly after this I began to learn what poverty meant. Dreadful days came when my father took the last of his webs to the great manufacturer, and I saw my mother anxiously awaiting his return to know whether a new web was to be obtained or that a period of idleness was upon us. It was burnt into my heart then that my father, though neither "abject, mean, nor vile," as Burns has it, had nevertheless to

> Beg a brother of the earth
> To give him leave to toil.

And then and there came the resolve that I would cure that when I got to be a man. We were not, however, reduced to anything like poverty compared with many of our neighbors. I do not know to what lengths of privation my mother would not have gone that she might see her two boys wearing large white collars, and trimly dressed. . . .

During my childhood the atmosphere around me was in a state of violent disturbance in matters theological as well as political. Along with the most advanced ideas which were being agitated in the political world — the death of privilege, the equality of the citizen, Republicanism — I heard many disputations upon theological subjects which the impressionable child drank in to an extent quite unthought of by his elders. I well remember that the stern doctrines of Cal-

vinism lay as a terrible nightmare upon me, but that state of mind was soon over, owing to the influences of which I have spoken. I grew up treasuring within me the fact that my father had risen and left the Presbyterian Church one day when the minister preached the doctrine of infant damnation. This was shortly after I had made my appearance.

Father could not stand it and said: "If that be your religion and that your God, I seek a better religion and a nobler God." He left the Presbyterian Church never to return, but he did not cease to attend various other churches. I saw him enter the closet every morning to pray and that impressed me. He was indeed a saint and always remained devout. All sects became to him as agencies for good. He had discovered that theologies were many, but religion was one. I was quite satisfied that my father knew better than the minister, who pictured not the Heavenly Father, but the cruel avenger of the Old Testament — an "Eternal Torturer" as Andrew D. White ventures to call him in his autobiography. Fortunately this conception of the Unknown is now largely of the past.

One of the chief enjoyments of my childhood was the keeping of pigeons and rabbits. I am grateful every time I think of the trouble my father took to build a suitable house for these pets. Our home became headquarters for my young companions. My mother was always looking to home influences as the best means of keeping her two boys in the right path. She used to say that the first step in this direction was to make home pleasant; and there was nothing she and my father would not do to please us and the neighbors' children who centered about us.

My first business venture was securing my companions' services for a season as an employer, the compensation being that the young rabbits, when such came, should be named after them. The Saturday holiday was generally spent by my flock in gathering food for the rabbits. My conscience reproves me to-day, looking back, when I think of the hard bargain I drove with my young playmates, many of whom were content to gather dandelions and clover for a whole season with me, conditioned upon this unique reward — the poorest return ever made to labor. Alas! what else had I to offer them! Not a penny.

I treasure the remembrance of this plan as the earliest evidence of organizing power upon the development of which my material success in life has hung — a success not to be attributed to what I have known or done myself, but to the faculty of knowing and choosing others who did know better than myself. Precious knowledge this for any man to possess. I did not understand steam machinery, but I tried to understand that much more complicated piece of mechanism — man. . . .

With the introduction and improvement of steam machinery, trade grew worse and worse in Dunfermline for the small manufacturers, and at last a letter was written to my mother's two sisters in Pittsburgh stating that the idea of our going to them was seriously entertained — not, as I remember hearing my parents say, to benefit their own condition, but for the sake of their two young sons. Satisfactory letters were received in reply. The decision was taken to sell the looms and furniture by auction. And my father's sweet voice sang often to mother, brother, and me:

To the West, to the West, to the land of
    the free,
Where the mighty Missouri rolls down to
    the sea;

Where a man is a man even though he
    must toil
And the poorest may gather the fruits of
    the soil.

The proceeds of the sale were most disappointing. The looms brought hardly anything, and the result was that twenty pounds more were needed to enable the family to pay passage to America. Here let me record an act of friendship performed by a lifelong companion of my mother — who always attracted stanch friends because she was so stanch herself — Mrs. Henderson, by birth Ella Ferguson, the name by which she was known in our family. She boldly ventured to advance the needful twenty pounds, my Uncles Lauder and Morrison guaranteeing repayment. Uncle Lauder also lent his aid and advice, managing all the details for us, and on the 17th day of May, 1848, we left Dunfermline. . . .

My father was induced by emigration agents in New York to take the Erie Canal by way of Buffalo and Lake Erie to Cleveland, and thence down the canal to Beaver — a journey which then lasted three weeks, and is made to-day by rail in ten hours. There was no railway communication then with Pittsburgh, nor indeed with any western town. The Erie Railway was under construction and we saw gangs of men at work upon it as we traveled. Nothing comes amiss to youth, and I look back upon my three weeks as a passenger upon the canal-boat with unalloyed pleasure. All that was disagreeable in my experience has long since faded from recollection, excepting the night we were compelled to remain upon the wharf-boat at Beaver waiting for the steamboat to take us up the Ohio to Pittsburgh. This was our first introduction to the mosquito in all its ferocity. My mother suffered so severely that in the morning she could hardly see. We were all frightful sights, but I do not remember that even the stinging misery of that night kept me from sleeping soundly. I could always sleep, never knowing "horrid night, the child of hell."

Our friends in Pittsburgh had been anxiously waiting to hear from us, and in their warm and affectionate greeting all our troubles were forgotten. We took up our residence with them in Allegheny City. A brother of my Uncle Hogan had built a small weaver's shop at the back end of a lot in Rebecca Street. This had a second story in which there were two rooms, and it was in these (free of rent, for my Aunt Aitken owned them) that my parents began housekeeping. My uncle soon gave up weaving and my father took his place and began making tablecloths, which he had not only to weave, but afterwards, acting as his own merchant, to travel and sell, as no dealers could be found to take them in quantity. He was compelled to market them himself, selling from door to door. The returns were meager in the extreme.

As usual, my mother came to the rescue. There was no keeping her down. In her youth she had learned to bind shoes in her father's business for pin-money, and the skill then acquired was now turned to account for the benefit of the family. Mr. Phipps, father of my friend and partner Mr. Henry Phipps, was, like my grandfather, a master shoemaker. He was our neighbor in Allegheny City. Work was obtained from him, and in addition to attending to her household duties — for, of course, we had no servant — this wonderful woman, my mother, earned four dollars a week by binding shoes. Midnight would often find her at work. In the intervals during the day and evening, when household cares would permit, and my young brother sat at her knee threading needles and waxing the thread for her, she recited to him, as she had to me, the gems of Scottish minstrelsy which she seemed to have by heart, or told him tales which failed not to contain a moral.

This is where the children of honest poverty have the most precious of all advantages over those of wealth. The mother, nurse, cook, governess, teacher, saint, all in one; the father, exemplar, guide, counselor, and friend! Thus were my brother and I brought up. What has the child of millionaire or nobleman that counts compared to such a heritage?

William Miller: MEN AT THE TOP — A "WASP" ELITE

Not only the propaganda of writers like Carnegie, but the work of historians helped to keep alive for years the "rags-to-riches" strand of the American Dream — the belief that America's great businessmen came from poor, immigrant, rural, uneducated families, devoid of social advantages, and that they grew rich by rigid adherence to the Calvinist ethic of hard work, thrift, chastity, and abstinence. Since World War II new research has undermined this belief. A large role in this revision

Reprinted by permission of the publishers from *Quarterly Journal of Economics*, "The Recruitment of the American Business Elite," by William Miller, Vol. LXIV, No. 2 (May, 1950), Cambridge, Mass.: Harvard University Press, Copyright, 1950, by the President and Fellows of Harvard College.

has been played by the free-lance historian William Miller (1912–   ). Educated at New York University and Columbia, Mr. Miller has worked at Harvard's entrepreneurial research center; taught at Yale, Columbia, and Michigan State; and served as an editor at Alfred Knopf and of Fortune magazine. Co-author of a leading textbook, he has also written a best-selling paperback on American history, a book-club selection of 1958. His article systematically weakens each link in the "rags-to-riches" argument, and makes us reconsider more carefully the origins of the Robber Barons.

ALMOST twenty years ago, Professors F. W. Taussig and C. S. Joslyn published their book, *American Business Leaders: A Study in Social Origins and Social Stratification.* Although its appearance was without doubt a landmark in the study of the subject, it is the opinion of the present writer that it has won its reputation, at least in part, by default: there simply have been no other studies of comparable scope in the social origins of American business leaders. Of the few articles that have appeared, none has been addressed directly to Taussig and Joslyn's poblem of determining the relative importance of heredity and environment in business success, and none has undertaken to test their conclusions.

My opinion that this book, while original and still useful, is limited in its achievement is supported by leading, if forgotten, reviews that appeared soon after its publication. That by Professor Morris Ginsberg in the *Economic Journal* speaks for many of the others. Professor Ginsberg said at the close of his review that "a study such as that made in the work before us, compelled as it is to confine itself to gross differences in the environment, and completely ignoring psychological and genetic analysis, cannot, it seems to me, hope to establish any reliable conclusions in a matter so intricate and complex as the share of genetic differences in social stratification."

The present paper, concerned with a generation of business leaders earlier than that studied by Taussig and Joslyn, but in objective rather more modest than their work, is one of a series aimed at extending our knowledge at least of the social characteristics of such men. In the first of these, I took issue with the description of the origins and upbringing of the "typical" American business leaders of the period since the Civil War that appears in those few American history books that have said anything at all about them. That description is virtually always of the "poor immigrant" or "poor farm" boy who, barely entering his teens, first found work in the meanest of jobs and, "fired by a passionate will to succeed," rose from "obscure origins" and "from poverty to riches" mainly "by dint of unflagging industry and resourcefulness." In my analysis of 190 of the topmost American business leaders in the first decade of the twentieth century, however, poor immigrant and poor farm boys together are shown to have made up no more than three per cent of this group. The great majority was recruited from higher status families and among themselves shared still other social characteristics.

In this paper the question to be discussed is: to what extent were these shared social characteristics found in large segments of the general population; to what extent were they found among the common run of people with whom business leaders by their own pronouncements on their origins have so often sought to identify themselves, yet over whom they have come to exercise great power?

II

In all classes of society and in all geographical, national, and religious groups in the United States in 1900 there must have been many adults who had not aspired to business eminence. If these could be separated from the rest of the people — and account be taken of them as a group apart — a population of aspirants would remain. This would be a better group than the whole population to compare with the business elite. For here it would be possible to point to the known failures as well as to the successes, and to identify more confidently and examine more closely than is now practicable the social conditions attending disappointment and achievement.

Needless to say, this division of the population cannot be made. In lieu of it, however, one may point to certain social groups in the population which, whether aspiring to business eminence or not, failed altogether to be represented among the topmost business bureaucrats discussed here.

"It was too bad women didn't count in Guggenheim business affairs," writes Harvey O'Connor, the biographer of the Guggenheim family, "for many said that Gladys was the most capable of [Daniel Guggenheim's] children." Their failure to use female talent, of course, scarcely made the Guggenheims unique. Females made up almost 49 per cent of the total population of the United States in 1900 and 47.5 per cent of those 50 years of age — the average age that year of the 190 business leaders. But these figures only make them one of the largest of the absent groups.

About 12 per cent of the population of the United States in 1900 was non-white — Negro, Indian, Mexican, Oriental; of the 50-year-old males that year, such non-whites were 16.2 per cent. None, however, are found among these elite businessmen. Also unrepresented are southern and eastern Europeans and their descendants, but they were only a relatively small proportion of the whole population. Sizable numbers of men from European countries south and east of Germany had begun to settle in the United States by 1880, but by 1900 they and their adult offspring as yet accounted for only about two per cent of the adult white population. Another small fraction of the population, made up of white immigrants and their descendants, from South America, Asia, Africa, and the islands of the seas, also are missing from the business elite.

These unrepresented national and racial minorities, however small in some instances, are worth mentioning if only for the sake of completeness of presentation. But there is also a better reason. Though their absence from the group studied here may be due simply to the smallness of this group, it may also point up other conditions governing elite recruitment, conditions suggested by the ascent of men from minorities actually represented in the group under view — notably the ascent of Jews.

Although in 1850 Jews accounted for only a small fraction of one per cent of the white population of the United States and although by 1900 their share had not yet risen much above one per cent, six of the business leaders studied here, or about three per cent of those whose religious heritage is known, were of Jewish descent — a better than average showing if it may be supposed that it would remain the same in a much larger sample. None of these six Jews, however, was in a non-Jewish firm. All attained the high positions that make them eligible for this study not only in Jewish enterprises but in those started by their fathers or other relatives.

It is the operation of this factor in particular, this apparent tendency toward religious and national and even family segregation within the business elite — shown as much by the failure of most firms to recruit for their executive hierarchies members of religious or national minorities, as by the practice of men in such minorities, when in power, of favoring their own people — which seems to be indicated most sharply by the history of the absent minorities. Among the latter there appears to have been no one as yet to affirm that their normal lower class goals could be transcended, no one to serve as a model for their sons' or their compatriots' aspirations, and, perhaps most important, no one to serve as the direct instrument of their ascent.

It is worth noting, too, that the envelopment by 1900 of many of the key areas of the economy by the extant business bureaucracies must have made the outlook all the more restricted for those seemingly excluded at once from these bureaucracies and from those key areas in which almost alone great business success could be won.

III

Published census information being what it is for the period of the lives of the men studied here, many distinctions less subtle than that between aspirants and nonaspirants to great business success also are impractical. In only a few categories, for example, can information on the 50-year-old white males in the population, as of 1900, be separated out from that on the population as a whole. In the following pages, where informa-tion on this age and sex group is unavailable, less exclusive comparisons are made between the business leaders and the population generally; and where census data are altogether lacking, other sources are used.

The twelfth census, 1900, does report the birthplaces of the population insofar as they may be identified as native or foreign, by sex, color, and age groups. These figures reveal a considerable disproportion between the foreign-born among all 50-year-old white males and the foreign-born in the business elite under view, those in the first group comprising 34.8 per cent, those in the second only 10 per cent. This census also reports on parents' birthplaces and shows that of all 50-year-old white males, 45.6 per cent had at least one foreign-born parent. Those of foreign-born or mixed parentage in the business elite make up only 19 per cent. It appears, therefore, that as many as four out of five among the business bureaucrats studied here, as against only slightly more than half of the 50-year-old white males generally, were native-born of native parents.

Predominantly of old American families, these business bureaucrats naturally were largely of British descent, 79 per cent of them tracing their origins to England, Scotland, the north of Ireland and other places in the British Empire, exclusive of the south of Ireland. Exactly how this proportion compares with that among the 50-year-old white males in 1900, or even with that in the population as a whole, is difficult to determine. Satisfactory estimates of the national origins of the American people are available only for 1790 and 1920. These are presented in Table 1, together with the national origins of the business elite.

The proportion of persons of British (exclusive of south Irish) descent in the

TABLE 1

National Origins of the American Population and of the Paternal Lines of the Business Elite

Country[a]	American Population, 1790[b] (Per Cent)	American Population, 1920[c] (Per Cent)	Business Elite Born about 1850 (Per Cent)
England and Wales	60.1 ⎫	⎫	53 ⎫
Scotland	8.1 ⎪	⎪	7 ⎪
North of Ireland	5.9 ⎬ 74.1	4.14[d] ⎬ 47.2	11 ⎬ 79
Canada	e ⎪	5.6 ⎪	3 ⎪
British Empire, other or unspecified	e ⎭	.2 ⎭	5 ⎭
South of Ireland	3.6	11.2	3
Germany	8.6	16.3	12
Other Countries	13.7	25.3	6
Percentage Total	100.0	100.0	100.0
Numerical Total	3,226,944	94,821,000	162

[a] Last country before settlement of paternal family or businessman himself in colonies or the United States.
[b] American Council of Learned Societies, "Report of the Committee on Linguistic and National Stocks in the Population of the United States," in *Annual Report of the American Historical Association, 1931* (3 volumes, Washington, D. C.: Government Printing Office, 1932), I, p. 124.
[c] Thompson and Whelpton, *op. cit.*, p. 91. For explanation of why total cases in this column does not equal total population in 1920, see *ibid.*, p. 84.
[d] This includes England and Wales, Scotland, and north of Ireland.
[e] Numbers too small to count.

United States probably was never higher subsequent to 1790 than it was that year, while the proportions of those of south Irish and of German descent probably were never lower. Thus, the excess of the first group in the business elite in 1900, as compared to the proportion of this group in the population even in 1790, would appear to indicate a sizable over-representation in the elite of persons of British (exclusive of south Irish) ancestry. A comparison, on the other hand, of the estimates of persons of south Irish and of German origin in 1790 and 1920 with the relative size of such groups in the business elite, seems to disclose a marked under-representation in the elite of persons of such ancestry.

This seeming disproportion in the elite in favor of persons descended from the *national* majority appears to be somewhat reversed in the statistics on *religious* heritage. Here again only approximations are available. The twelfth census, 1900, does not report the religious composition of the 50-year-old white male group. The census of 1850, in turn, the one nearest the median year of birth of the business elite, reports only "church accommodations," that is, the seating capacity of the buildings used for worship — probably only a rough index of the actual size of the religious bodies in the United States that year. A comparison of these figures with those on the religious affiliations of the business elite discloses in the latter a somewhat above normal representation of Catholics and Jews (though the numbers involved are small) at the expense of the Protestant majority in general. The greatest differences between the elite and the population, however, as Table 2 shows, appear to be in the under-representation of the largely middle and lower

TABLE 2
*The Religious Heritage of the American Population
and the Business Elite*

Denomination[a]	American Population, 1850[b] (Per Cent)		Business Elite[c] (Per Cent)		
Episcopal	4.5	} 19.1	25	} 46	30[d] } 55
Presbyterian	14.6		21		25
Methodist	30.5	} 53.2	9	} 14	11 } 17
Baptist	22.7		5		6
Unitarian	1.0		6		7
Other Protestant	22.0		8		11
Protestant, Unspecified	00.0		16		—
Total Protestant	95.3		90		90
Roman Catholic	4.6		7		7
Jewish	.1		3		3
Percentage Total	100.0		100		100
Numerical Total	14,270,139		174		174

a In almost all instances this is the religion of the businessman himself, though most likely of his father too. In the few instances in which a shift is known to have occurred, the old religion only is counted.
b Based on seating capacity of buildings used for worship. Actual total reported is about 61.5 per cent of the entire population, 1850. See J. D. B. DeBow, *Statistical View of the United States* (Washington: A. O. P. Nicholson, 1854), pp. 136–137.
c All the businessmen about whom this information is known are included here, native-born as well as foreign-born. The distribution of religions among the latter is not sufficiently different from that for the whole group to affect the figures as shown in any significant way.
d This column shows the distribution of the business leaders by religious denomination, on the assumption, safe enough it seems, that the "Protestant unspecified" group was distributed in the same proportions as the known specified Protestant.

class Protestant denominations, Methodist and Baptist, and the over-representation of Episcopalians and Presbyterians, denominations more often associated with higher status.

IV

The immediate surroundings in which these great business bureaucrats were raised probably were as important in shaping their careers as were their national and religious inheritances in opening such careers to them.

Since these men not only were of old American families, but were businessmen as well, they might be expected to have come not from the farms but largely from the older commercial and industrial sections of the country. And so they did,

indeed even in greater proportions than would normally be expected. Sixty-one per cent of the native-born among them originated in New England and the Middle Atlantic states, which area should, statistically speaking, have supplied only about 39 per cent. These figures and the others for the population generally, in Table 3, are based on reports of births in the seventh census, 1850.

Even more striking, in comparison to the distribution of the whole population in 1850, is the proportion of the business elite born or raised in the business atmosphere of American cities and larger towns.

Statistics on the occupations of the American population or any large segment of it in the nineteenth century are

TABLE 3

Native-Born Business Leaders and Native-Born Free Population
by Region of Birthplace

Region[a]	Whites and Free Negroes Born in the United States, 1850[b] (Per Cent)	Native-born Business Elite (Per Cent)
New England	11⎫	20⎫
Middle Atlantic	28⎰ 39	41⎰ 61
East North Central	25	25
South	31	10
West	5	4
Percentage Total	100	100
Numerical Total	548,837	169

[a] These are census regions. Combined in "South" are South Atlantic, East South Central, West South Central; in "West," West North Central, Mountain, and Pacific states and territories.
[b] DeBow, *op. cit.*, p. 111. Though free Negroes are combined with whites in the census tabulation, there were not enough of them, even were their regional distribution much different from that of the whites, to alter materially the distribution as shown.

TABLE 4

Business Leaders by Size of Birthplace or Place where Raised
and the American Population by Size of Community

Size of Community	American Population, 1850[a] (Per Cent)	Business Elite[b] (Per Cent)
City (over 8,000)	12.5⎫	41⎫
Town (2,500 to 8,000)	4.3⎰ 16.8	19⎰ 60
Rural (under 2,500)	83.2	40
Percentage Total	100.0	100
Numerical Total	23,191,876	170

[a] Thompson and Whelpton, *op. cit.*, p. 20.
[b] The size used here for each man's place of birth or upbringing is its size according to the census nearest the man's year of birth, not the census of 1850. Place of upbringing is used for all men who moved, before the age of seven, to places sufficiently larger or smaller than their birthplaces to alter their classification in the scale used in this table.
Of the 18 foreign-born business leaders, six who were brought to the United States before the age of seven and raised here are included in this tabulation. Of those excluded, only one was born in a rural place; most of the others were born in great cities.

scanty, and those that are available, especially for the period before 1870, are notoriously unreliable. Still, none of the earlier ones suggest the need for any revision of the impression of an extraordinary concentration in the business elite of men with business family backgrounds, an impression given by the geographical origins of these men as compared with the geographic distribution of the population generally. Occupational statistics for 1870, in turn, are close enough to the period when the men in the business elite were being raised and launched on their business careers to afford relevant comparisons with the occupations of the fathers of these men. And the 1870 occupational data only strengthen the conclusions drawn from those on regional and city-size origins.

TABLE 5

*Occupations of American Males and the Fathers
of the Business Elite*

| Occupationa | American Males, 1870 | | Fathers of the Business Elite (Per Cent) |
	Taussig and Joslynb (Per Cent)	C. Wright Millsc (Per Cent)	
Businessman	6.2	8.1	56 ⎱ 86
Professional	2.5	2.3	30f ⎰
Farmer	32.0	28.2 ⎱ 58.7	12
Rural Worker	⎱ 56.7d	61.4 ⎰ 30.5 ⎰	0
Urban Worker	⎰	⎱ 30.9	2
Other	2.6	e	e
Percentage Totals	100.0	100.0	100
Numerical Totals	9,420,000	11,007,505	167

a "Professional" includes independent as well as salaried men; most of those among the fathers of the businessmen were lawyers, engineers, or men engaged in politics, even if not always office holders. "Urban worker" includes wage as well as lower salaried occupations, manual as well as clerical and sales jobs.
b From F. W. Taussig and C. S. Joslyn, *op. cit.*, p. 273.
c This distribution is adapted from *White Collar: The American Middle Class* (Oxford University Press, 1951) by Professor C. Wright Mills, who was generous enough to permit me to use his occupational data before the book's publication.
d Taussig and Joslyn do not distinguish between rural and urban workers.
e Only Taussig and Joslyn use this miscellaneous category.
f In my earlier paper, where a comparison of the backgrounds of business and political leaders was made, this figure appeared as only 23 per cent, for the 7 per cent of these business leaders whose fathers were public officials were listed separately. Here it seemed sensible to include them with professionals.

Two summaries of 1870 occupational statistics are given in Table 5, together with the occupations of the fathers of the business elite. As shown there, well over half of these fathers were businessmen. Business and professional men together make up a remarkable 86 per cent.

These occupational statistics must make it clear that, as compared to the American population generally, few of the business leaders under discussion were born or raised in lower class families. The fact that, in a period when most American boys went to work very early in life, only 20 per cent of these business leaders had business jobs before they were sixteen, only strengthens this conclusion. It gains more strength still from statistics on education. In an age when the educational level of the American population generally certainly was no higher than elementary school graduate, only 22 per cent of these business leaders had terminated their formal schooling at that point. Thirty-seven per cent could point to a high school education or its equivalent. The remaining 41 per cent had gone to college, approximately three out of four of them graduating. How far this 41 per cent exceeded the proportion of college men in the population generally is indicated by the following statistics. In 1870, the census year nearest that in which most of these college-educated business leaders would have been in attendance, there were in the United States 2,067,144 white males between the ages of 15 and 20. That year there were 67,350 males in the colleges and universities of the country — a scant 3.3 per cent of the white males of college age.

v

If it be true, as leading American businessmen and leading American historians continue to assert, that, so to speak, anyone can become president of large business firms, it appears to be true also that at least in the early twentieth century most of the successful aspirants had certain social characteristics that distinguished them sharply from the common run of Americans of their time. Such distinguishing characteristics may have been less marked among American business leaders in the first half or three-quarters of the nineteenth century, though too little is known about that period to generalize with safety. In the bureaucratic twentieth century, however, many of these characteristics were so prevalent among the business leaders, and so rare among the rest of the population, that the presumption, at least, is strong that they constituted genuine advantages in the competition for business eminence.

III. THE ROBBER BARONS AS PIRATES

RAILROADS AND RAILROADING

James Bryce: THE RAILROAD KINGS — AMERICA'S GREATEST MEN

James Bryce (1838–1922) was a famous English viscount, scholar (professor of civil law at Oxford, 1870–93), statesman (a Liberal M.P. who held various cabinet posts), man of letters, student of American affairs, and onetime British ambassador to Washington (1907–13). He wrote in the Robber Baron era a shrewd and detailed commentary on the United States political system, The American Commonwealth *(1888). This distinguished study, despite its flaws, has stood the test of time and ranks with Alexis de Tocqueville's* Democracy in America *(1835) as one of the very few major interpretive works on American politics. In the brief extract below, Lord Bryce sketches in a few words the rise to power of the Railroad Kings. For him the Robber Barons seemed to be reasserting in America "the principle of monarchy."*

A WELL-ESTABLISHED company has sometimes to apprehend a peculiarly annoying form of attack at the hands of audacious adventurers, who construct a competing line where the traffic is only sufficient to enable the existing one to pay a dividend on the capital it has expended, aiming, not at the creation of a profitable undertaking, but at levying blackmail on one which exists, and obtaining an opportunity of manipulating bonds and stocks for their own benefit. In such a case the railway company in possession has its choice between two courses: it may allow the new enterprise to go on, then lower its own rates, and so destroy all possibility of profits; or it may buy up the rival line, perhaps at a heavy price. Sometimes it tries the first course long enough to beat down the already small prospects of the new line and then buys it; but although this may ruin the "pirates" (as they are commonly called) who have built the new line, it involves a hideous waste of the money spent in construction, and the shareholders of the old company as well as the bondholders of the new one suffer. This is a form of raid upon property which evidently ought to be prevented by a greater care on the part of State legislatures in refusing to pass special Acts for unnecessary railroads, or in so modifying their law as to prevent a group of promoters from using for purposes of blackmail the powers of taking land and constructing railroads which general statutes confer.

This atmosphere of strife has had something to do with the feature of railway management which a European finds most remarkable; I mean its autocratic character. Nearly all the great lines are controlled and managed either by a small knot of persons or by a single man. Sometimes one man, or a knot of three or four capitalists acting as one man, holds an

From James Bryce, *The American Commonwealth,* Vol. II (London, 1888), pp. 512–516, abridged.

actual majority of the shares, and then he can of course do exactly what he pleases. Sometimes the interest of the ruling man (or knot) comes so near to being a controlling interest that he may safely assume that no majority can be brought against him, the tendencies of many shareholders being to support "the administration" in all its policy. This accumulation of voting power in a few hands seems to be due partly to the fact that the shares of new lines do not, in the first instance, get scattered through the general public as in England, but are commonly allotted in masses to a few persons, often as a sort of bonus upon their subscribing for the bonds of the company. In the United States shares do not usually represent a cash subscription, the practice being to construct a railway with the proceeds of the bonds and to regard the shares as the materials for future profit, things which may, if the line be of a speculative character, be run up in price and sold off by the promoters; or, if it be likely to prosper, be held by them for the purpose of controlling as well as gaining profits from the undertaking. It is partly also to be ascribed to the splendid boldness with which financial operations are conducted in America, where the leaders of Wall Street do not hesitate to buy up enormous masses of shares or stock for the purpose of some *coup*. Having once got into a single hand, or a few hands, these stock masses stay there, and give their possessors the control of the line. But the power of the railways, and the position they hold towards local governments, State legislatures, and one another, have also a great deal to do with the phenomenon. War is the natural state of an American railway towards all other authorities and its own fellows, just as war was the natural state of cities towards one another in the

ancient world. And as an army in the field must be commanded by one general, so must this latest militant product of an eminently peaceful civilization. The president of a great railroad needs gifts for strategical combinations scarcely inferior to those, if not of a great general, yet of a great war minister — a Chatham or a Carnot. If his line extends into a new country, he must be quick to seize the best routes, — the best physically, because they will be cheaper to operate, the best in agriculture or mineral resources, because they will offer a greater prospect of traffic. He must so throw out his branches as not only to occupy promising tracts, but keep his competing enemies at a distance; he must annex small lines when he sees a good chance, damaging them first so as to get them cheaper; he must make a close alliance with at least one other great line, which completes his communications with the East or with the farther West, and be prepared to join this ally in a conflict with some threatening competitor. He must know the Governors and watch the legislatures of the States or Territories through which his line runs; must have adroit agents at the State capitals, well supplied with the sinews of war, ready to "see" leading legislators and to defeat any legislative attacks that may be made by black-mailers or the tools of rival presidents. And all the while he must not only keep his eye upon the markets of New York, prepared for the onslaught which may be made upon his own stock by some other railroad or by speculators desiring to make a profit as "bears," and maintaining friendly relations with the capitalists whose help he will need when he brings out a new loan, but must supervise the whole administrative system of the railroad — its stations, permanent way, locomotives, rolling stock, engineering shops, freight and passenger rates, perhaps also the sale of its land grants and their defence against the cabals of Washington. No talents of the practical order can be too high for such a position as this; and even the highest talents would fail to fill it properly except with a free hand. Concentration of power and an almost uncontrolled discretion are needed; and in America whatever commercial success needs is sure to be yielded. Hence, when a group of capitalists own a railway, they commit its management to a very small committee among themselves, or even to a single man; and when the shares are more widely distributed, the shareholders, recognizing the necessary conditions of prosperity, not to say of survival in the struggle for existence, leave themselves in the hands of the president, who has little to fear except from the shares being quietly bought up by some syndicate of enemies seeking to dethrone him.

Of these great railway chieftains, some have come to the top gradually, by the display in subordinate posts of brilliant administrative gifts. Some have begun as financiers, and have sprung into the presidential saddle at a bound by forming a combination which has captured the railway by buying up its stock. Occasionally a great capitalist will seize a railroad only for the sake of manipulating its stock, clearing a profit, and throwing it away. But more frequently, when a really important line has passed into the hands of a man or group, it is held fast and developed into a higher efficiency by means of the capital they command.

These railway kings are among the greatest men, perhaps I may say are the greatest men, in America. They have wealth, else they could not hold the position. They have fame, for every one has heard of their achievements; every newspaper chronicles their movements. They

have power, more power — that is, more opportunity of making their personal will prevail — than perhaps any one in political life, except the President and the Speaker, who after all hold theirs only for four years and two years, while the railroad monarch may keep his for life. When the master of one of the greatest Western lines travels towards the Pacific on his palace car, his journey is like a royal progress. Governors of States and Territories bow before him; legislatures receive him in solemn session; cities and towns seek to propitiate him, for has he not the means of making or marring a city's fortunes? Although the railroad companies are unpopular, and although this autocratic sway from a distance contributes to their unpopularity, I do not think that the ruling magnates are themselves generally disliked. On the contrary, they receive that tribute of admiration which the American gladly pays to whoever has done best what every one desires to do. Probably no career draws to it or unfolds and develops so much of the characteristic ability of the nation; and I doubt whether any congressional legislation will greatly reduce the commanding positions which these potentates hold as the masters of enterprises whose wealth, geographical extension, and influence upon the growth of the country and the fortunes of individuals, find no parallel in the Old World.

It may be thought that some of the phenomena I have described belong to an era of colonization, and that when the West has been filled up, and all the arterial railways made, when, in fact, the United States have become even as England or France, the power of railroads and their presidents will decline. No doubt there will be less room for certain bold ventures and feats of constructive strategy; and as the network of railways grows closer, States and districts may come to depend less upon one particular company. At the same time it must be remembered that the more populous and wealthy the country, so much the larger the business of a trunk line, and the number of its branches and its employés; while the consolidation of small lines, or their absorption by large ones, is a process evidently destined to continue. It may therefore be conjectured that the railroad will long stand forth as a great and perplexing force in the economico-political life of the United States. It cannot be left to itself — the most extreme advocate of *laissez faire* would not contend for that, for to leave it to itself would be to make it a tyrant. It cannot be absorbed and worked by the National government; — only the most sanguine state socialist would propose to impose so terrible a strain on the virtue of American politicians, and so seriously to disturb the constitutional balance between the States and the Federal authority. Many experiments may be needed before the true mean course between these extremes is discovered. Meanwhile, the railroads illustrate two tendencies specially conspicuous in America, — the power of the principle of association, which makes commercial corporations, skilfully handled, formidable to individual men; and the way in which the principle of monarchy, banished from the field of government, creeps back again and asserts its strength in the scarcely less momentous contests of industry and finance.

Matthew Josephson: JAY GOULD — CLASSIC VILLAIN

Can we distinguish between "good" and "bad" Robber Barons? Among the "worst" have always been placed a group of railroad speculators — Cooke, Drew, Fisk, and Gould. Here Jay Gould (1836–1892) is examined by Matthew Josephson (1899–   ), a distinguished professional writer. After graduating from Columbia, Mr. Josephson worked for ten years as an editor (at one time on the New Republic*), before becoming a full-time free-lance writer. Besides* The Robber Barons, *excerpted here, he has written a dozen books ranging over United States political history (*The Politicos, 1865–1896 [1938] *for example), biography (*Zola, Stendahl, *and others), and reminiscences (*Life Among the Surrealists [1962]*). His biography of Edison won the Parkman Prize in 1960. In 1934, at the height of the Depression, Josephson portrayed Gould as "the Mephistopheles of Wall Street."*

WHILE the productive labors of a society, the functioning of its ships and railroads, its mills and factories, give the effect of a beautiful order and discipline, of the rhythmic regularity of the days and seasons, its markets, by a strange contrast, seeem to be in a continual state of anarchy. Here the same services and commodities, produced every day with perfect routine, go through a mad dance. The market, as Marx has pointed out in a striking passage, is like a "city without a plan." Yet only in the market can the capitalist take his reward. Here he must move without a faltering step under pain of instant destruction. He must tell none what his plans are; he must smile or remain impassive when he is in torment or danger. For his business is difficult, laborious and risky. He must show infinite resourcefulness, efficiency, sagacity. He must, as Marx states it,

have fine hearing and a thick skin; must be simultaneously cautious and venturesome, a swashbuckler and a calculator, careless and prudent. He must, in fine, develop all the qualities of an experienced man of business.

By this definition of the man of the market, Jay Gould seems the capitalist par excellence. During all the heroic, turbulent period we review he seems the very soul of the movement of industrial revolution; he shows the "purest" traits, if one may call them so, of the great entrepreneur.

Where certain of his rivals, intoxicated with power, learned to crave glory too, Jay Gould seemed to place himself above such human vanities. Nor did any social interest, or any sentimental consideration, as of the size or beauty of an enterprise, deflect him for a moment from his marvelously logical line of movement. No human instinct of justice or patriotism or pity caused him to deceive himself, or to waver in any perceptible degree from the steadfast pursuit of strategic power and liquid assets. Others, such as Rockefeller and Morgan, had their friendships, personal loyalties to colleagues or members of their class. Gould, who had only *agents* rather than confidants or allies, seemed to enjoy most the rôle of "the one against all"; self-contained, impassive to all pleas or reproaches, he seemed content with his loneliness. For most of his days he lived, as it has been said of Harriman, who resembled him so much, "in the necessary isolation of a ship's commander when on sea duty." At times he seemed to soar above the others like a destroying angel.

What would he have done, or rather what great works would he have *undone*, if his health had not failed him? He lived in the agony of a consumptive, not daring to admit his infirmities for fear of the enemies always ranged against him. While plunged in his large designs, he would pass nights without sleeping, coughing blood in terrible spasms, walking the street outside his home until dawn. He died prematurely, in the midst of life, and his vast unknown plans foundered with him.

In all the things he did, he seemed pervaded with a demoniac pessimism, which in sober retrospect does him much honor. There were certain developments which must have filled him with an enduring mistrust of the very system which he exploited so brilliantly. At the height of his career, after the Civil War, the commodity markets of the world seemed to resume their prolonged downward trend, which they had shown ever since the Napoleonic wars. The earth, in these years, from its civilized states and wildest colonies seemed to belch forth a torrent of goods; the armies of labor were constantly multiplied; and new inventions, new machines appearing with bewildering rapidity added to abundance and cheapness incessantly, while making obsolete existing machinery and destroying fixed capital. Hence what appears to others a wanton destructiveness in Gould, his intermittent raids or attacks, were but testing operations carried on against a system he may have believed fore-doomed. Thus possessed of terrible doubts, he was constantly turning his supposed advantages in securities, or goods, into ready money; assumed gains, surplus value, in perpetually renewed campaigns must be turned into cash. He never deceived himself.

He was a small man, weak in physique, and he loved power — the realities of power rather than its vestments. "I did not care at that time about the mere making of money," he said with reference to his sensational exploits in the Missouri Pacific Railroad. "It was more to show that I could make a combination and make it a success."

The giant size of a project, the dangers it offered, the speed and skillful precision with which it must be carried out — all this stirred his strange imagination. Since his boyhood he had dreamed of making a transcontinental railroad; and now in 1873, free of the Erie, he had begun to buy shares of the celebrated Union Pacific. Its stock of $100 par value had sunk to $30 after the Crédit Mobilier scandal; then even to $14. He continued buying.

"I found myself a very large owner in that property," he admitted to a committee of United States Senators some years later. "Then . . . I found that there was ten millions of bonds that came due in a month or two. . . . It was rather a blue condition of things."

When Daniel Drew had parted company with him in 1868, he had jeered: "There ain't nothing more in Erie." But Gould and Fisk had shown him a trick or two. So with Union Pacific. Though looted, the tremendous line which took days to traverse suited perfectly the bold

plans being formed by the Mephistopheles of Wall Street.

In accordance with his large designs, one broken railroad after another was quickly taken over by Gould throughout the Middle West and the Southwest. From Thomas Scott, whom he found "very much broken up, financially, physically and mentally," he acquired a working interest in the Texas and Pacific, which had been chartered in 1871 to run between Galveston and San Diego, but was virtually unbuilt. From Scott also he purchased an important newspaper, the *New York World*. Then he reached for fragments of defunct railroads, franchises, land grants about to be forfeited. These included the ill-fated Kansas Pacific (which had gained great subsidies in land and money), now fallen into receivership; the Denver Pacific, the Wabash, the Missouri Pacific, all of which, together with connecting and feeding lines, gridironed the West. Then, by effecting favorable transfer agreement with Collis Huntington, he would gain an outlet to the sea via California. In the meantime, the Pacific Mail Steamship Company was acquired by him in conjunction with Huntington to keep ocean carrying-rates by way of Panama from competing with the land crossing. To these properties he was to add, by systematic raids, the rich telegraph monopoly of the Western Union Company; then the new rapid-transit lines being built in New York to carry her millions back and forth to their unremitting labor; finally a series of coal mines; and toward the end, railroads running to the Eastern seaboard, to round out an industrial empire which spread its crazy network from one shore of the continent to the other.

The railroads, the telegraph lines, the ships, the newspapers, all were part of an imperial plan to capture strategic sections of the country's industrial system, and, by blocking it first at one point, then at another, to levy infinite toll upon it.

To understand the scope of the man's tactics one must note that his domination was carried on by strategic "working controls" rather than by ponderous outright investments. He was an "absolute master," as a shrewd investigator for President Cleveland reported, "of the art of creating coördinate boards of directors that had complete control of adverse interests." Thus the ruin of certain properties which he controlled at slight expense might be turned to his own pecuniary gain. All his tactics, therefore, hinged upon what Thorstein Veblen has defined as "disturbance of the industrial system." He would pursue a deliberate policy of mismanagement "as a matter of principle," deriving his gains from the discrepancies between the real value of the affair and its supposed or transient value in the security markets. In good times he would give an appearance of gauntness and misery to his enterprise; in bad times he would pretend affluence. Sin and weakness were simulated when he was buying control; "prosperity," when he longed to sell out. At all times, from his position of vantage, he would be as one who deals out marked cards in the game of buying and selling capital, since he would be fully able to foresee the "nature, magnitude and incidence" of all the risks he created. His system could no more fail than loaded dice.

Moreover, his analysis of the railroad prospects of the Great West was an uncommonly penetrating one. With his unsentimental eye he saw at once that it was useless to engage in a legitimate shipping and passenger business while waiting for the thinly settled prairies to fill up. Nothing justified the present building and operation of large railroad

systems save that other entrepreneurs would do so if he did not. And though there would be no adequate volume of freights to support such ventures, one must be beforehand in seizing the strategic positions essential to a future monopoly. Thereafter, there were only two ways of making the operation pay: by owning an unchallenged monopoly of a given territory and "charging all the traffic would bear" (though this was not certainly profitable); or by manipulation of its capital in the markets — and none knew how to do this better than Jay Gould. When the structure collapsed, Jay would be somewhere else. Then it must be set up again. . . .

Students of these affairs have sometimes questioned the social value of Gould's labors. Disappointed investors, the hard-pressed public which perforce patronized his lines, often cursed his name as that of an evil genius. But he would have answered: "We are not in business for our health!" Every tactical advantage must be translated quickly into cash, to be used again in new ventures. Those who did not imitate Jay Gould, or did not go as far as he did, probably learned to regret their error.

One becomes impersonal when at the head of mighty corporate enterprises; one does not feel at close hand the disillusionment or ill-will of the customers, as one might in the days of guilds and mercantile capitalism; one is even less sensitive when one regards the customers as an inferior class. . . .

The Missouri Pacific, upon which the State of Missouri once lavished $25,000,-000 in subsidies, had fallen into the railroad baron's hands for $3,800,000, . . . This line he kept for himself. By diverting traffic to it, adding small connecting roads, building extensions, and "growing up with the country," he soon erected a system that ran over 5,000 miles of track from St. Louis west to Omaha, and southwest to El Paso.

He was ever afterward proud of his "constructive labor" in the Missouri Pacific's territory. The railroad's receipts had risen twentyfold during his management, he was apt to boast. "We," he added passionately, boastfully, "have made the country rich, we have developed the country, coal mines and cattle raising, as well as cotton. . . . We have created this earning power by developing the system." He believed this, as Harriman and other railroad monarchs after him believed that they built the country and its wealth, they had "made the Great West!"

Gould clung to the Missouri Pacific as to no other property, with a certain sentiment; it was to remain as a family heirloom down to quite recent years. But loving this railroad he could not help raping it occasionally, as he did the Wabash, and so many others. Under favorable reports, made by extraordinary accounting devices which none else might control, he would raise the value of his stocks, sell, depreciate, and repurchase them. So the Wabash, which had but little traffic or reason for existence at the time, and which was mismanaged with "trained incompetence," as Thorstein Veblen would say, its treasury empty, its stock maintained by secret loans at a high price — the poor Wabash was to crash in a sensational débâcle, in which it appeared afterward that Jay Gould was in no way involved. He was simply not there when it happened.

The Missouri Pacific too paid dividends "by curtailment of necessary repairs and replacements," its stock price remaining high in the face of a mounting deficit. Wherever Gould moved or struck upon the map of the country, "the effects of his management never wore off entirely," observes Riegel in his "History of the Western Railroads":

There was never any effort to build up a strong, soundly managed group of roads . . . the one dominant note was speculation. Both in prosperity and depression he pursued his aim shrewdly and relentlessly. . . . The roads that he touched never quite recovered from his lack of knowledge and interest in sound railroading.

. . . In the immediate vicinage the roving dark eyes of Gould soon distinguished toward 1881 a new and golden opportunity, a new prize to contest for. The City of New York was having its first rapid-transit system developed, in the shape of the steam-driven elevated railways; and two companies, the Manhattan Elevated and the New York Elevated Railway Company, were in the field. He saw the future of this property and in 1881, after he had seized the telegraph combination, determined to have possession of it. Here is one of his most famous financial exploits, one that may be regarded as the most brilliant of his last period.

After studying the problem for some time he concluded that in order to buy the properties cheaply for himself, as in the Western Union case, he must harass and block the present management at every turn, he must make them wretched in mind and body, he must convince the owners that their investment was a ruinous one.

At first he attacked the Manhattan Elevated through the courts, and his procedure may be followed day by day in the newspaper he controlled. On May 18, 1881, Attorney General Ward, acting upon information he possessed, appeared before a justice of the New York State Supreme Court and asked leave to begin suit on behalf of the people to annul the charter granted to the Manhattan Elevated Railway. At the same time, the *New York World,* in its editorial and financial columns, carried on a tirade against the existing owners, suggesting that the company was insolvent and that its directors were guilty of conspiracy. In the meantime, over the telegraph wires which Gould owned, garbled despatches and strange rumors were circulated in all directions.

From a level of 57 the stock of Manhattan Elevated soon fell to 29, although the condition of the company appeared actually most promising. Now Gould and Sage began buying the stock while the attacks of the *World* and a battle of writs and injunctions kept the price at weak or "reasonable" levels. In Gould's office at the Western Union Building, Judge Westbrook of the Supreme Court (formerly Gould's legal counsel) prepared a petition in bankruptcy for the unhappy traction company.

But once Gould's party had taken over a major share of the stock, the price of Manhattan Elevated advanced, smiles spread everywhere and, miracle of miracles, the company was found to be sound and solvent. The *New York World,* after a five months' campaign, seemed appeased. It reported on October 18, 1881:

Manhattan Elevated opened today at 45, sold down to 37, and closed at 43, the recovery following the announcement of an agreement between the elevated companies . . . [we have] never believed but that Manhattan would be rescued by men who have the brains and the means to make the most of it.

Jay Gould was now in charge of the company which owned the first two elevated railways in New York. Among those who helped him reach this point was Cyrus Field, one of the original stockholders, who had conspired with him ever since the Erie days, 1871. But Field was a distinguished man, originator of the submarine cables; he was socially prominent and known as a powerful, enthusiastic leader in speculations and investments. He thought at first that it would be well to work closely with Gould, rather than otherwise; he made a good front, and became titular head of the Manhattan Elevated Railways.

Once in command of the city's elevated railroads, Gould, Sage and Field issued more capital, manipulated their shares upward, raised the passenger fares, and harvested rich profits. However, all was not as well as it seemed. In portions of the press, especially in the then crusading *New York Times,* Gould was subjected to heavy bombardment; he was a "scourge," a "pirate," a "corrupter of public servants," the Devil in human guise. The *Times* declared:

There is no more disgraceful chapter in the history of stock jobbing than that which records the operations of Jay Gould, Russell Sage, Cyrus W. Field and their associates in securing control of the system of elevated railroads in New York City.

Such animadversions would have mattered little to the deep little man, as accustomed to the malice of his rivals as to the envy of those whom he defeated in the race. Mr. Field, however, the tall, white-bearded social lion among the trio, who had been the willing instrument of Gould, was nettled by the attacks. He showed curious symptoms of a public conscience; he sought to defend himself or make amends in some form. To the great vexation and disgust of Gould, Field, as the titular head of the Manhattan Elevated, determined to lower the passenger fares from ten to five cents, announced that he considered his company an institution for the public service and the development of his city — not to speak of his own large landholdings — and carried a faction among the stockholders over to his side.

To Gould's mind — as a pure tactician of capitalism — nothing could have been more insane and wasteful than such a policy, which conflicted seriously with his own ingenious plans for the treatment of New York's transportation system. It ran counter to all his usual schemes for planned mismanagement or derangement, such as opened the way to the pecuniary results he desired. And when Field used his resources to buy large blocks of stock in his railroad and reenforce his control, Gould determined to be rid of the "reformer" in their midst.

Together with Sage, he laid his snares stealthily. They waited for the good moment to strike — as the bravo with his stiletto waits for his victim to turn his back. They encouraged Field to buy, while they sold him their stock. When, by all their vehicles of information, they knew that Field was "overloaded," they fell upon the market in one of their catastrophic raids. Field's credit collapsed and the price of Manhattan Elevated broke almost in half. He was ruined but Gould "rescued" him, by consenting to take over his encumbered securities at a sacrifice to Field of many millions, "a state of things which Gould was generally accused of having produced."

The circumstances of this affray were unusually pathetic and lingered long in the public mind through rumor and report. Mr. Field, previous to his association with Gould, had been of high moral repute, a popular citizen engaged apparently in some public-spirited enterprises which happened to be useful to land and building developments. He was, moreover, the father of several beautiful and gifted daughters, one of whom, in her memoirs, described the sad chute of their gorgeous household, which came at a time when Mr. Field's health was sinking. So destitute did he become in the end that money was raised for him by sympathetic friends such as J. P. Morgan, and his last years seem to have been passed in long mental and physical anguish.

The successful outcome of this business with Manhattan Elevated and Field enhanced for Gould a reputation which in certain aspects was awkward. He was at the height of his temporal power; buying and selling, building and tearing down great railway systems, over a territory between the Mississippi, Missouri and Colorado rivers. He operated in a country which exceeded in dimensions Germany, Italy, France and Spain combined; he employed directly every day more than one hundred thousand men; while as an early biographer admiringly reports, "his word was law throughout the vast interest in his control established in many states and territories — almost from ocean to ocean." No man in the United States possessed more power than Mr. Gould, it was said; and none enjoyed more luxury than he, whether upon his yacht, the *Atalanta*, with its carved furniture and rare tapestries, or in his queer gingerbread Gothic castle outside of the city, at Irvington-on-Hudson.

Among the masses themselves, awe and terror spread of his power. What could be done with a man who controlled the press service and telegraph system as well as railroads, a man who could read all minds, scan all secrets, form opinion and rumor, hasten or delay events? In 1884, during the stormy contest for the presidency between Blaine and Cleveland, it was charged that Gould was holding back the election returns which passed over Western Union wires, either in the interests of Blaine, or to secure himself from loss in the market in the event of Cleveland's success. A mad crowd filled the streets, threatened to sack the Tribune Building, and then surged before the massive Western Union Building, singing:

Hang Jay Gould to a sour-apple tree!

It was strange music. Imperturbable as ever, Gould reported the next day, on being questioned, that he had been at his country home nursing a cold and consoling himself in his greenhouse among the thousands of the largest orchids in the world, which he cultivated as his chief hobby.

The workers themselves combined against him in 1884 and 1885 under the belligerent and somewhat ritualistic banner of the Knights of Labor; their strikes, attended with unprecedented destruction and bloodshed, were heavy blows. Yet even such assembled might, such collective force, was vain to overcome him.

On the whole he retained his extraordinary composure through these trying events. His face was a mask, his eyes, "glowing like coals" but even and calm of glance, seldom revealed the fearful tension under which he labored, the agonized nights, the fatigue, the racking illness and pain borne successfully by his supremely vigorous spirit, which in another time would have been equal to the most heroic exploits. Always he must remain unhurried, soft-spoken. None must know and none knew his ways and movements. Only one instance was generally heard of when his guard was lowered. He was ill, but appeared with his doctor at a directors' meeting. Here the unexpected opposition of his old partner Russell Sage caused his nerves suddenly to snap, and precipitated a scene of hysteria, from which his doctor led him raving to his bed.

It was at this time that the hosts of enemies he had gained began to gather together to plot his downfall, modeling their tactics and general procedure after the methods of the great money-master himself. In the ceaselessly troubled precincts of Wall Street, these mercenary soldiers, who could seldom trust each other with their backs turned, were all united against him. Their repeated conspiracies against Gould formed some of the most romantic legends of the Street. In 1881 a great storm blew down the wires of his telegraph companies. Gould was at this time compelled to use a messenger-boy service and the brokers, Cammack and Travers, kidnaped his boy and replaced him with a spy who resembled him. For days the spy brought Gould's most secret communications to the enemy headquarters at the Windsor Hotel, where they were opened and then sent on to their proper destinations. Grievous losses came to Gould in this manner before he discovered the ruse.

In 1882, at the time of the spectacular collapse of his Southwestern railroads, his credit was attacked; rumors were spread that he was heavily in debt to banks and must soon unload masses of securities he held upon a declining market. Calling witnesses to his office, he had his private secretary bring bundles of bonds and stock from his vault and displayed them. There were $53,000,000 of securities which he possessed outright, and much more elsewhere, he declared. Thus it was seen that he had been mysteriously forewarned and had completely escaped the ruin of his own railroad enterprises.

Two years later renewed attacks, timed with the general financial depression, undoubtedly brought him to the edge of danger. Men whose financial life he had apparently taken years before revived to fill the ranks of his enemies; James Keene, his former partner, Henry N. Smith,

Charles Woerishoffer, a celebrated plunger who died young, and many other Wall Street leaders united to "break" Gould at the time of the Grant and Ward panic in 1884, when his railroads were falling in ruins and he was thought to be heavily laden. He attempted to support the market against heavy onslaughts. But day by day he was brought lower; his Missouri Pacific, his Western Union, everything he owned was hammered down to bankruptcy levels. The unbelievable thing happened. Jay Gould was beaten. Halstead relates:

One morning he had his lawyer execute an assignment of his property, and on the following day — a beautiful Sunday morning — his yacht went down to Long Branch where the bear operators were summering. Gould's emissaries landed and held a conference with his foes. They bore his ultimatum — a copy of the assignment and a statement that unless the bears made terms with him he would on the following morning . . . give public notice that he was unable to meet his engagements.

According to the obscure allusions of his biographer, he had assigned a portion of his unencumbered holdings so that it would remain to his heirs. Officially he, in person, would descend into bankruptcy to the extent of millions. And his failure would create a far greater panic than that which was now raging, one in which the very concerns with which the bears had contracts would founder in the universal crash, making them, too, heavy losers. Thus, like Samson, he stood ready to tear down the house in which they all lived. The bears after long conference agreed to "let up" on terms of receiving 50,000 shares of Western Union at 50, which they had sold much higher. They expected him to fail in any event soon after.

But Gould now used the very money they released in order to turn upon them and smite them hip and thigh. He cornered his Missouri Pacific and other stocks in which his adversaries were short, trapped them and forced them to stand and deliver. Once more he had miraculously escaped from the fate he prepared for so many others.

Nevertheless he was deeply alarmed by the near-catastrophes of 1884–85. More prudent in his last years, he husbanded his reserves until his war chest was ample once more. Then after several years of comparative armistice, he would assume the offensive again. At the very hour of his death in 1892 he would be bent upon new campaigns of conquest, as vast, as impenetrable as ever.

Julius Grodinsky: JAY GOULD — CAPITAL CREATOR

By 1957 the advancing tide of revisionism in history had reached even Jay Gould. In his fresh look, Julius Grodinsky (1896–1962) did not try to wash out all Gould's alleged former sins, lavishly described by Matthew Josephson and others. But, as befits an economist who specialized in corporation finance and taught it for many

From Julius Grodinsky, *Jay Gould, His Business Career, 1867–92* (Philadelphia, 1957). Reprinted by permission of the University of Pennsylvania Press.

years at the University of Pennsylvania, Professor Grodinsky took a cool and dispassionate view of his subject, and found reason to emphasize the creative side of Gould's financial genius — the building up of America's social overhead capital in railroads, for instance, and the overall reduction in railroad rates that ensued.

IN assessing the importance of a business leader, his contribution to the industry and to the public welfare must be considered. This is particularly true in an examination of business success in the free-enterprise economy of the period following the Civil War. Argument is still hot between those who deny and those who defend that system as the best means of affording to the community a high standard of living. Although it is probable that the unregulated capitalistic economy of the nineteenth century has been weakened, there is still no agreement upon the extent to which a regulated economy can exist without destroying the profit motives which make a free-enterprise system possible.

It is therefore particularly profitable to examine the contributions made both in terms of business advance and public service which were made by Gould in the generation following the Civil War. Gould was, and still remains, a business type. He had his virtues and he had his faults. His defects have been exaggerated beyond their true significance. Gould possessed a cold-blooded unscrupulousness which enabled him to take full advantage of the primitive nature of the art of corporate finance and the status of corporate law, and to adapt to his purpose the low state of political morals prevailing at the time.

What positive contribution did he make to the transportation and telegraph industries with which for the better part of his business life he was so closely associated? What contribution did he make to the well-being of the general public? How did he promote the general interests of the community? To many conservative businessmen of the time, interested primarily in the promotion of stability and in the maintenance of the earnings of well-established enterprises, Gould was a wrecker of existing value, "a destroyer of the peace," to use the language of one of the careful businessmen of the time. He sold stocks short to depress their value and then frequently outwitted his short-selling associates by buying them back at low prices, even while his associates were still selling. This he did on a large scale with the Western Union Telegraph, and on a smaller scale with other corporations. He made contracts not to build railroads into the territories of his rivals, only to violate them when it was profitable for him to do so. He made rate agreements only to break them. He issued statements on security values merely to confute his opponents in the stock markets.

Strange to say, these very misstatements and continuous violations of the spirit if not of the letter of the contracts, enriched his contribution to the public welfare, even though they impaired, at least temporarily, the earning power of a large section of the railroad industry. Perhaps even stranger is the circumstance that the very factors which temporarily injured the industry, did in fact over the longer period aid it, and enhanced both its permanent value and its long-term earning capacity. Gould's violation of the understandings prohibiting the building of new roads, for example, led to the extensive rate wars which depressed rates and reduced railroad earnings. The reduction of dividends in 1884 and 1885 by eastern, and in the late eighties by western, railroads followed by the extensive receiverships in the early and middle nineties, were largely the result of the rate wars and the promiscuous building of new railroads. Yet the reduction in rates was of extraordinary benefit to consumers and producers. Although the immediate effects were disastrous to corporate earnings, the long-range effects were beneficial, not only to shippers and consumers but also to the railroads themselves. The depressed rates increased operating efficiency and lowered costs. This paved the way for a rise in traffic made possible in part by reduced rates. The lowered rates were permanent. The traffic and managerial alliances and understandings of the middle nineties and of the first decade of the present century, and the waves of railroad consolidations and acquisitions, did not produce any substantial rate increases.

It is however necessary to point out that for a part of his career, Gould was instrumental in raising rates. His acquisition of control of the Union Pacific, possessing the only transcontinental route of the seventies, was followed by the introduction of monopolistic policies. In the depression of the middle and late seventies, transcontinental rates over the combined Central Pacific-Union route were raised sharply through the united efforts of Huntington and Gould. Also, discriminations between shippers, classes of traffic, and geographical areas were imposed in order to increase railroad earnings.

Except for this phase of his career Gould, in quest of business advantages for the companies with which he was associated, fought for reduced rates. Together with McHenry, he was the leading factor in the reduction of rates on crude and refined oil that brought the cost of oil transportation down to the low levels of the late sixties and early seventies. Rockefeller took advantage of the railroad competition that Gould and McHenry initiated in order to exact the maximum business concessions for his refineries, and rates thus reduced were not increased. In fact the rate structure on the petroleum traffic was further corroded in the following decades. Gould's control of the Erie railway was also featured by the rate battles with Commodore Vanderbilt.

The most far-reaching effects on the railroad rate structure, however, were reflected in 1879 and in the eighties, following Gould's brilliant expansion program. In these years he repeatedly broke up rate structures and territorial agreements. He furthermore destroyed established rate and traffic pools in rapid succession. From 1879 until the late eighties, when the pursuit of this policy brought earnings and stock values to the lowest point attained since the late seventies, he consistently followed this policy of intransigence. His activities produced widespread business unsettlement and contributed to the creation of a group of foes who characterized him as a corporate wrecker and business disturber.

Aside from his association with the Erie, Gould first instituted this policy in a major sense soon after he gained control of the Wabash. In one incident after another he took the aggressive. The rate depression in the Missouri Valley and in the Middle West was due in considerable degree to his policies.

The invasion of southern Iowa by the Wabash in 1880; the construction by the Missouri Pacific of the line to Omaha in 1881; the ill-concealed extension into the

Atchison territory in southern Kansas through the instrumentality of a partially controlled subsidiary; the invasion of the Leadville territory in Colorado through the Union Pacific; and the elaborate construction and expansion program in the Southwest — all contributed in the late eighties to the largest railroad-building program and to some of the most violent rate wars in American railroad history.

When Gould initiated his policy of rate-cutting and railroad construction in 1879, competitive railroad relationships in many parts of the country had become reasonably well stabilized. Gould broke up this stabilized rate and territorial structure. The eventual result was the construction of the Burlington's line to Denver, and the emergence of competition with the Union Pacific on transcontinental traffic. The rate wars that followed the Burlington invasion of the Union Pacific territory permanently reduced rates. The same results followed in eastern and central Kansas, where the Atchison eyed closely the Gould invasion of its lucrative traffic-producing country. The Gould aggression was partly responsible for the Atchison's counter-measures, primarily the construction of the Kansas City-Chicago extension and the transformation of the road into a new transcontinental system. Again, to use another example, the conflict of Gould with the Gulf was followed by the merger of that property with the Atchison. With the aid of additional construction in Oklahoma, this union produced a new competitive through route between the Missouri Valley and the Gulf Coast.

By reducing rates with apparent abandon as a means of achieving results, Gould impaired the fortunes not only of his competitors but also those of his own properties. Though the security holders of many roads may have lost, the public

was a major gainer. The record building construction in 1879–81 and in 1886–87 were in part the consequence of competitive fears inspired by the Gould policies. Gould was in this sense a public servant. The building program in the eighties, of the Atchison, the Union Pacific, the Burlington, the Rock Island, the Northwestern, and the St. Paul, reflected to a considerable degree adjustments to his rate-cutting, business-disturbing policies.

Although in this sense Gould rendered a public service, he accomplished nothing in the raising of railroad service standards or in reducing costs. His roads during his lifetime and for two generations thereafter had an unsavory reputation. To the operating man accustomed to efficient car and train movements and to the shipper accustomed to expeditious deliveries, the Gould railroads were by no means a blessing. A Gould road in the Southwest was a byword for poor service. To the operating man and shipper the poor service of a Gould road was compared with the good service of the Atchison. . . . The Gould roads were poorly maintained; in fact usually drastically undermaintained. And an undermaintained railroad cannot render a high standard of service.

Neither did Gould introduce any mechanical improvements in the railroad industry nor for that matter in the telegraph industry. Gould was no inventor and had no mechanical ability; and unlike Westinghouse, for example, he made no contribution to the mechanical arts of the day. He had none of the driving genius for new and better things which characterized the activities of Rockefeller and Carnegie.

Having thus considered his accomplishments in one field, and his failings in another, attention must be directed now to another phase of his business activity in which the truth lies hidden in a complex business and financial organization. Gould throughout his life was attacked by group after group of security holders. From the beginning of his experience with the Erie it was his destiny to be associated with properties which had passed through receivership and reorganization. Except for the Union Pacific, and also for the Lackawanna in which he had only a minority interest, every major transportation property with which he became associated had a history of financial reverses. To an extent this was true even of the Union Pacific. Although the road had not gone through receivership prior to Gould control, the price of its securities had fallen to low levels and its original promoters after suffering heavy financial losses had lost control. The other properties prior to Gould control had either been in, or had narrowly escaped, receivership. The Kansas & Texas, the International, the Iron Mountain, the Texas & Pacific, the Denver, the Kansas Pacific, the Wabash, the Hannibal, and a number of smaller lines which were acquired by the larger properties were included in this category. Many of these roads after a number of years under Gould control drifted back into the receiverships from which they had so recently emerged. The drop in the market value of their securities which accompanied their financial embarrassment was usually laid to the evil genius of Gould. He was the scapegoat of the unsuccessful, as were the bankers and the utility magnates in the depression of the 1930's, and the Federal Reserve Board in 1920 and 1921.

To some extent this conclusion was justified. Gould in promoting rate wars and in invading local territories occupied by other railroads contributed to the financial difficulties of many roads and to that extent security holders were correct in ascribing their losses to Gould. The complaints of the losers were loud and long, and were registered in the daily press and in other organs of public opinion. They were also reflected in the documents presented before the courts and legislative committees by opponents of Gould and his policies. It is clear that losses were incurred and it is therefore easy to conclude that those who followed Gould lost money, and that the loss inflicted by the Gould policies represented a loss to the community.

This conclusion, however, does not represent the entire truth. To arrive at a conclusion reflecting financial and economic realities, it is essential to examine the source from which capital necessary for expansion in a dynamic capitalistic society is derived. The flow of capital into the production of goods and services necessary to meet consumer demands was only slightly affected in the seventies and eighties by governmental policies. The process of capital creation thus reflected the free play of economic influences. Gould operated largely in the railroad industry in which the demand for capital was exceptionally heavy. Except for a limited number of companies, the funds needed for the construction of new roads were secured by the sale of bonds and stocks. Funds were secured in part from individual and institutional savings. Such a source of capital creation is normal and this supply in conjunction with the demand for capital from borrowers produces what economists call a "natural" rate of interest. There are, however, other methods of creating purchasing power essential to capital formation. Expenditures by government for capital purposes out of the proceeds of bond issues sold to the banks became a normal feature in the 1930's and 1940's. Whatever objection there may be to this practice, the fact remains that billions of dollars of capital expenditures have been thus financed.

Purchasing power for capital improvements is also created by changes in capital values. The nature of these values and the extent to which they contribute to the growth of capital in a capitalistic economy should be properly appraised. Those who take the lead in creating capital from this source are frequently condemned as speculators or as the recipients of unearned gains. These profits are on occasion exceptionally large, although the losses under adverse economic conditions are even larger. Since the number who are successful in this phase of business are relatively few, there seems to be a presumption of inequity, or perhaps even of dishonesty, by those who are successful. This hypothesis may be a major reason for the failure to examine this problem adequately and to assess the contribution made by participants in this field of business to the public interest in a capitalistic economy.

A rise in the market value of assets consisting either of land and its improvements, or of stocks and bonds representing the capitalized earnings realized from the use of land and improvements thereon, produces an increase in the purchasing power of the holders of such property rights. Some of the holders may have bought such rights at one price level and held them throughout the period when they sold at a lower price level, awaiting their return to the original, higher cost level. To those people the increase in market value from the lower price level may represent no increase in purchasing power. There are others, however, who purchase securities at the low prices prevailing normally in a period of depression. It may be contended that the buyers gain only that amount which the sellers lose. This does

not necessarily follow. Those who sell the securities have already made their contribution to the economic well-being of the community. The cash they paid for their securities or for other evidence of property rights has already been expended by the borrowers and transformed into capital. The capital exists in the form of railroads, telephone, telegraph, machines, or tools which are creating services for the consumer. The new security purchasers make additional commitments. Their investments are not transformed immediately into capital formation. Such investments transfer purchasing power to the original holders, who have now become sellers. To determine the economic benefits to the community coming from the increased capital values, it is essential to consider the disposition made of these greater values on the part of buyers. If the buyers hold the securities through the rising capital market; if, that is to say, they never sell the securities they have made no important contribution to the public welfare.

The buyers of the securities at the depression-made low prices may, however, sell their securities at the high capital values established in the boom era. When the securities are converted into cash, the purchasing power of the holders is correspondingly increased. If that purchasing power is then transferred to those businessmen who are active producers for transformation into capital goods, then a substantial economic benefit has been realized. If the holders sell their securities at high prices and use the proceeds to buy new securities directly from the corporations which use the cash to install capital improvements, the productive wealth of the community is increased.

Those who buy and sell such securities in periods of low and high prices, respectively, are frequently described as speculators or as suppliers of "equity" capital. The first is a questionable and the second a praiseworthy description of the functions of the role of this kind of capital creator in the period of recovery from a general depression. It is then generally recognized that fixed charges have become too heavy for many corporations to carry. What is needed under these conditions, it is therefore contended, is capital which carries no interest charges. In the later stages of cyclical recovery, in the midst of an economic boom, the services of the supplier of equity capital are not so generally recognized since by that time funds for capital needs are relatively easy to obtain. Conservative people, particularly those representing financial institutions such as banks and insurance companies, stimulated as they are by a record of good earnings over a period of years, are willing to provide capital yielding low returns. This is especially true if such returns are fixed contractually in terms of dollars. The borrowing corporations in turn are desirous of making such contracts. They can thereby make substantial profits from the difference between the interest paid and the profits expected to be realized from the use of the borrowed funds. Those who buy stocks at high prices in the latter stages of a boom and who lose part of their capital are frequently described as speculators; while those who buy at low depression prices and sell at the high boom prices are frequently described as investors. Ordinarily those who have not bought the securities at the low depression prices are so impressed by the record of boom-time earnings, presumably so well established as to insure their indefinite continuance, that they are led to buy the securities at the higher boom prices.

Those who followed Gould in the purchase of securities at the low depression-born prices and in the early period of recovery, made exceptional profits. It is perhaps not so clear, however, that those who made these gains were not so voluble in their praise as were those who were so expansive in seeking a scapegoat for their losses. Gould above all was a leader in the field of speculative capital and in this phase of business activity he performed a service to society. It was also in this field that he made his greatest personal gains and contributed most to the public weal. In this field he did not, however, realize the maximum potential gains. He made many mistakes, as do most businessmen in this and other fields. In the early recovery from the depression lows of 1877 he was on the wrong side of the market and his short sales produced heavy personal losses. After the successful resumption of specie payments in January, 1879, he changed his mind. He financed his early buying ventures by the sale of a substantial block of Union Pacific stock to the Sage-Keene syndicate. His purchases in the spring and summer of 1879 [included] the Kansas Pacific, Wabash and other securities, which he bought at an accelerated tempo. . . . In his buying program, it is an established fact that Gould had a large following. Sage, Humphreys, (S.) Dillon, Field, Tilden, G. M. Pullman, Marquand, J. S. Seligman, Keene, Woerishoffer, Sloan, T. A. Scott, W. L. Scott and Hopkins, among many others, participated with him in the purchase of securities at depression prices. Each of these capitalists had his own following, and though it is not possible to establish the extent of the group that followed his leadership, it is a reasonable assertion that their numbers could be counted in the thousands.

Gould also had a following abroad, particularly in Holland, where his purchase of Denver & Pacific bonds in the summer of 1879 created a favorable impression among capitalists. As early as 1875, his leadership in reversing market trends by using Union Pacific stock as a vehicle, created much good feeling there.

Aside from the Union Pacific stock, the securities which Gould purchased on a large scale in 1879 and 1880 had little investment following. Although the roads responsible for the issue of these securities were strategic from the standpoint of their importance to the economic life of the community, they had yielded slight returns to the original investors. Since they were financially weak, their properties were in poor physical condition. It is therefore not surprising that conservative capitalists, such for example as Forbes, referred to these properties contemptuously as the "broken-down" railroads. The prices of these securities were exceptionally low. Gould's market judgment in 1879 and 1880 was excellent, and those who followed his lead realized substantial profits. It is of more than passing significance to observe that those capitalists who were associated with Gould in these two luscious years were not among his bitter critics. Among his followers during this period were a number, Woerishoffer for example, who later disagreed with him on the problems of market trading. Woerishoffer gained and Gould lost in the panic markets of May, 1884, whereas Gould profited and Woerishoffer lost by reason of Gould's sale of his Denver stock and the failure of Woerishoffer to sell his in the booming markets of 1881. Neither man condemned the other because of his market losses.

. . . In these years, characterized by a rapid expansion in the nation's productive plant, thousands of miles of railroads were built by the Gould roads. Few of these properties enjoyed a high credit rating. They therefore had to finance their needs in the speculative markets. Gould was a leader in this field, and hundreds of communities owed their early facilities to his speculative leadership. A substantial portion of the speculative funds employed in the building of new lines came from those who had reaped capital gains from the purchase and sale of Gould securities. The reorganization of the Texas & Pacific in the mid-eighties, for example, disclosed the large number of Pennsylvania citizens who followed the lead of Scott and Gould in the purchase of its securities. Tilden, Marquand, Field, and Sage were heavy buyers of securities sold to finance railroad construction. The volume of Gould railroad mileage built during the first part of the boom of the eighties was by no means inconsiderable. Taking the four-year period of 1879–82, inclusive, as a basis for study, the new mileage built by the Wabash-Kansas & Texas-Missouri Pacific-Iron Mountain-International-Texas & Pacific-and Union Pacific systems (excluding the Lackawanna, where the building of the Buffalo extension was also financed to a great extent by capital of Gould and his following) amounted to 4,231.29 (See Table I). Assuming a cost of $20,000 per mile,

Miles of Road Built by Gould Railroads 1879–1882
TABLE Ia
(Excludes construction in Republic of Mexico)

1. Texas Pacific	1,010.00
2. Union Pacific	1,249.87
3. Wabash	462.01
4. International Great Northern	256.71
5. Missouri Kansas & Texas	588.2
6. Missouri Pacific	466.5
7. St. Louis Iron Mountain & Southern	198.0
	4,231.29

a The mileage of the first three roads is based on letters from these companies. The mileage of the last four is based on data in Poor's *Manual of Railroads*.

probably on the low side in the strong commodity markets in the early eighties, this construction involved an investment of $84,620,000.

A substantial part of the funds invested in the stocks (and bonds) of the Gould railroads in the early eighties was later lost. Similar losses flowing from investment in state government bonds sold to finance public works in a boom period were incurred in the wake of the panic of 1837, and far more extensive losses were inflicted from time to time by default and repudiation of European governments as the result of disastrous wars and even more disastrous peace treaties. There is, however, a notable difference between the nature and the distribution of the losses from private securities as contrasted with those from government securities. Risks in the former group are assumed and losses absorbed by the investor. Except for government subsidies, the investor cannot transfer the loss to any other group; he assumes the risk and either takes the profits or absorbs the loss. Losses arising from improper financing of government needs, however, are usually taken by the taxpayer. It is only in the event of the destruction of the government or of a breakdown in the economy, that the investor is forced to take the loss either in the form of default or repudiation, or in the guise of a worthless currency in which the debt is repaid.

Except for the destruction of a country's economy, or the devaluation of its currency, the issues of government bonds for nonproductive purposes thus remain a permanent liability upon the community. Bonds issued by corporations on the other hand are reduced or eliminated in the course of time as the unprofitable character of the capital in which the funds have been committed is revealed. So it was with many of the bonds of the Gould-controlled railroads — the Wabash, the Kansas & Texas, the International, and the Texas & Pacific during the lifetime of Gould, and those of the Missouri Pacific after his death. Some of the bonds were exchanged for stock. No longer was the public taxed to finance the payment of interest on an unproductive debt. The unproductivity of the debt in many cases was the result not of the economic disutility of the capital, but rather of the decline in railroad rates. That is to say, the unfortunate investment made by the bondholder gave the public a railroad facility at a low price. It was the combination of fixed capital which could be converted to no other use and of depressed rates that frequently undermined the safety of the investment. The security holders, followers of Gould, who sold at the top prices of 1881 realized good capital gains. Those who reinvested such gains in the Gould railroads eventually lost part. Distribution of profits and losses among Gould followers was highly unequal. While Sage for example invested a major part of his profits in railroad bonds which maintained their value even in depression, Field invested his in the stock of the Manhattan Elevated at high prices. His loss was fatal.

Whatever the loss of the followers of Gould and to Gould himself, the public benefited from his activities as a man of business in the railroad industry and in the field of speculative capital. As a leader in the railroad industry he built many new roads; he broke down local territorial monopolies, destroyed traffic pools, and wrecked railroad rate structures. As a leader in the arena of speculative capital, he transformed millions of dollars of paper profits into productive wealth in the form of new railroads. Gould made fortunes for many of his followers, and produced losses for others.

What his followers in the security markets gained, many did not permanently retain. The public did gain permanently, so far as anything permanent can be assumed to exist in economic life. Through the use of funds obtained from speculative followers and which could not have been obtained from investors, he built many new railroads. At the same time, in the process of disturbing existing business values, he reduced permanently the price of railroad service. To Gould, as much as to any other single business leader, goes the credit for that far-reaching reduction in rates that characterized the growth of the American economy in the generation after the Civil War.

TRICKS OF THE OIL TRADE: REBATES AND DRAWBACKS

Henry Demarest Lloyd: THE SOUTH IMPROVEMENT COMPANY — A "FIENDISH CONSPIRACY"

This further reading from Henry Demarest Lloyd, and the Allan Nevins selection which follows it, present two sharply different views of the South Improvement Company scheme of 1872. For the pre-Muckraker Lloyd, the Company was a "fiendish conspiracy" introduced by John D. Rockefeller into a previously prosperous industry in order to extract maximum personal profit at public expense. Lloyd implies that the scheme wrecked the oil industry. This chapter from his influential exposé of Standard Oil, Wealth Against Commonwealth *(1894), forms a major part of his indictment of Rockefeller. Its truth or falsity is therefore of crucial importance in helping you to decide the question: Robber Barons — pirates or pioneers?*

THE oil age begins characteristically. As soon as Drake's well had made known its precious contents [1859], horses began running, and telegrams flying, and money passing to get possession of the oil lands for the few who knew from those who did not know. The primitive days when "it was not monopolized by any one" were over. Thousands of derricks rose all over the territory, and oil scouts pushed with their compasses through the forests of the wilderness in all directions. Wells were bored all over Europe, as well as America, wherever traces of oil showed themselves, sometimes so close together that when one was pumped it would suck air from the other.

As soon as the petroleum began to flow out of the ground, refineries started up at every available place. They were built near the wells, as at Titusville and Oil City [Pennsylvania], and near the centres of transportation, such as Pittsburg and Buffalo, and near the points of export, as Philadelphia, Baltimore, New

From Henry Demarest Lloyd, *Wealth Against Commonwealth* (New York, 1894), Chapter V.

York. Numbers of little establishments appeared on the Jersey flats opposite New York.

There was plenty of oil for every one; at one time in 1862 it was only ten cents a barrel. The means of refining it had long before been found by science and were open to all; and even poor men building little stills could year by year add on to their works, increase their capital, and acquire the self-confidence and independence of successful men. The business was one of the most attractive possible to capital. "There is no handsomer business than this is," said one of the great merchants of New York. "You can buy the (crude) oil one week, and sell it the next week refined, and you can imagine the quantity of business that can be done." Men who understood the business, he said, "if they had not the capital could get all of the money they wanted."

Before the panic of 1873 — days of buoyant general prosperity, with no commercial revulsion for a cause — the citizens of this industry began to suffer a wholesale loss of property and business among the refineries in New York, Pittsburg, Cleveland, and elsewhere, the wells of the oil valleys, and the markets at home and abroad.

To the building of refineries succeeded the spectacle — a strange one for so new a business — of the abandonment and dismantling of refineries by the score. The market for oil, crude and refined, which had been a natural one, began to move erratically, by incalculable influences. It went down when it should have gone up according to all the known facts of the situation, and went up when it should have gone down. This sort of experience, defying ordinary calculations and virtues, made business men gamblers.

"We began speculating in the hope that there would be a change some time or other for the better," testified one who had gone into the business among the first, and with ample capital and expert skill.

Where every one else failed, out of this havoc and social disorder one little group of half a dozen men were rising to the power and wealth which have become the marvel of the world. The first of them came tardily into the field about 1862. He started a little refinery in Cleveland, hundreds of miles from the oil wells. The sixty and more manufacturers who had been able to plant themselves before 1860, when they had to distil coal into petroleum before they could refine petroleum into kerosene, had been multiplied into hundreds by the arrival of petroleum ready made from below. Some of the richest and most successful business men of the country had preceded him and were flourishing. He had been a bookkeeper, and then a partner, in a very small country–produce store in Cleveland. As described by his counsel some years later, he was a "man of brains and energy without money." With him were his brother and an English mechanic. The mechanic was bought out later, as all the expert skill needed could be got for wages, which were cheaper than dividends. Two or three years later another partner was added, who began life as "a clerk in a country store," and had been in salt and lumber in the West. A young man, who had been in the oil region only eleven years, and for two of the eleven had been errand-boy and bookkeeper in a mixed oil and merchandise business, a lawyer, a railroad man, a cotton broker, a farm laborer who had become refiner, were admitted at various times into the ruling coterie.

The revolution which revolved all the

freemen of this industry down a vortex had no sooner begun than the public began to show its agitation through every organ. The spectacle of a few men at the centre of things, in offices rich with plate glass and velvet plush, singing a siren song which drew all their competitors to bankruptcy or insanity or other forms of "co-operation," did not progress, as it might have done a hundred years ago, unnoticed save by those who were the immediate sufferers. The new democracy began questioning the new wealth. Town meetings, organizations of trades and special interests, grand juries, committees of State legislatures and of the United States Senate and House of Representatives, the civil and criminal courts, have been in almost constant action and inquiry since and because.

It was before the Committee of Commerce of the National House of Representatives in 1872 that the first authentic evidence was obtained of the cause of the singular ruin which was overwhelming so fair a field. This investigation in 1872 was suppressed after it had gone a little way. Congress said, Investigate. Another power said, Don't investigate. But it was not stopped until the people had found out that they and the production, refining, and transportation of their oil — the whole oil industry, not alone of the valleys where the petroleum was found, but of the districts where it was manufactured, and the markets where it was bought and sold, and the ports from which it was shipped abroad — had been made the subject of a secret "contract" between certain citizens. The high contracting parties to this treaty for the disposal of an industrial province were, on one side, all the great railroad companies, without whose services the oil, crude or refined, could not be moved to refineries, markets, or ports of shipment on river, lake, or ocean. On the other side was a body of thirteen men, "not one of whom lived in the oil regions, or was an owner of oil wells or oil lands," who had associated themselves for the control of the oil business under the winning name of the South Improvement Company.

By this contract the railroads had agreed with this company of citizens as follows:

1. To double freight rates.
2. Not to charge them the increase.
3. To give them the increase collected from all competitors.
4. To make any other changes of rates necessary to guarantee their success in business.
5. To destroy their competitors by high freight rates.
6. To spy out the details of their competitors' business.

The increase in rates in some cases was to be more than double. These higher rates were to be ostensibly charged to all shippers, including the thirteen members of the South Improvement Company; but that fraternity only did not have to pay them really. All, or nearly all, the increase it paid was to be paid back again — a "rebate." The increase paid by every one else — "on all transported by other parties" — was not paid back. It was to be kept, but not by the railroads. These were to hand that, too, over to the South Improvement Company.

This secret arrangement made the actual rate of the South Improvement Company much lower — sometimes half, sometimes less than half, what all others paid. The railroad officials were not to collect these enhanced freight rates from the unsuspecting subjects of this "contract" to turn them into the treasury of the railroads. They were to give them over to the gentlemen who called themselves "South Improvement Company." The "principle" was that the railroad was not to get the benefit of the additional charge it made to the people. No matter how high the railroads put the rates to the community, not the railroads, but the Improvement Company, was to get the gain. The railroads bound themselves to charge every one else the highest nominal rates mentioned. "They shall not be less," was the stipulation. They might be more up to any point; but less they must not be.

To pay money to the railroads for them to pay back was seen to be a waste of time, and it was agreed that the South Improvement Company for its members should deduct from the ostensible rate the amount to be refunded, and pay the railroads only the difference. Simplification could not go further. The South Improvement Company was not even to be put to the inconvenience of waiting for the railroads to collect and render to it the tribute exacted for its benefit from all the other shippers. It was given the right to figure out for its members what the tribute would amount to, and pay it to them out of the money they owed the railroads for freight, and then pay the railroad what was left, if there was any left. The railroads agreed to supply them with all the information needed for thus figuring out the amount of this tribute, and to spy out for them besides other important details of their competitors' business. They agreed to make reports every day to the South Improvement Company of all the shipments by other persons, with full particulars as to how much was shipped, who shipped, and to whom, and so on.

The detective agency thus established by the railroads to spy out the business of a whole trade was to send its reports "daily to the principal office" of the thirteen gentlemen. If the railroads, forgetting their obligations to the thirteen disciples, made any reduction in any manner to anybody else, the company, as soon as it was found out, could deduct the same amount from its secret rate. If the open rate to the public went down, the secret rate was to go down as much. For the look of things, it was stipulated that any one else who could furnish an equal amount of transportation should have the same rates; but the possibility that any one should ever be able to furnish an equal amount of transportation was fully taken care of in another section clinching it all.

The railway managers, made kings of the road by the grant to them of the sovereign powers of the State, covenanted, in order to make their friends kings of light, that they would "maintain the business" of the South Improvement Company "against loss or injury by competition," so that it should be "a remunerative" and "a full and regular business," and pledged themselves to put the rates of freight up or down, as might be "necessary to overcome such competition." Contracts to this effect, giving the South Improvement Company the sole right for five years to do business between the oil wells and the rest of the world, were made with it by the Erie, the New York Central, the Lake Shore and Michigan Southern, the Pennsylvania, the Atlantic and Great Western, and their connections, thus controlling the industry north, south, east, west, and abroad. The contracts in every case bound all the roads owned or leased by the railroads concerned. The contracts were duly signed, sealed, and delivered. On the oil business of that year, as one of the members of the committee of Congress figured out from the testimony, the railroad managers could collect an increase of $7,500,000 in freights, of which they were to hand over to the South Improvement Company $6,000,000, and pay into the treasury of their employers — the railways — only $1,500,000.

The contract was signed for the New York Central and Hudson River Railroad by its vice-president, but this agreement to kill off a whole trade was too little or too usual to make any impression on his mind. When publicly interrogated about it he could not remember having seen or signed it.

"The effect of this contract," the vice-president of the Erie Railway Company was asked, "would have been a complete monopoly in the oil-carrying trade?"

"Yes, sir; a complete monopoly."

Of the thirteen members of the South Improvement Company which was to be given this "complete monopoly," ten were found later to be active members of the oil trust. They were then seeking that control of the light of the world which it has obtained. Among these ten were the president, vice-president, treasurer, secretary, and a majority of the directors of the oil trust into which the improvement company afterwards passed by transmigration. Any closer connection there could not be. One was the other.

The ablest and most painstaking investigation which has ever been had in this country into the management of the railroads found and officially reported to the same effect:

"The controlling spirits of both organizations being the same."

The freight rates were raised as agreed and without notice. Rumors had been heard of what was coming. The public would not believe anything so incredible. But the oil regions were electrified by the news, February 26, that telegrams had been sent from railroad headquarters to their freight agents advising them of new rates, to take effect immediately, making the cost of shipping oil as much again as it had been. The popular excitement which broke out on the same day and "raged like a violent fever" became a national sensation. The Titusville *Morning Herald* of March 20, 1872, announces that "the railroads to the oil regions have already put up their New York freight from $1.25 to $2.84, an advance of over one hundred per cent." Asked what reason the railroads gave for increasing their rates, a shipper said, "They gave no reason; they telegraphed the local roads to put up the rates immediately." This advance, the superintendents of the railroads told complaining shippers, had been made under the direction of the South Improvement Company, and they had been instructed to make their monthly collections of oil freights from that concern.

The evidence even seems to show that the South Improvement Company was so anxious for the dance of death to begin that it got the freight agents by personal influence to order the increased rates before the time agreed upon with the higher officials. Strenuous efforts were made to have the public believe that the contracts, though sealed, signed, delivered, and put into effect, as the advance in rates most practically demonstrated, had really not been put into effect. The quibbles with which the president of the South Improvement Company sought to give that impossible color to the affair before the committee of Congress drew upon him more than one stinging rebuke from the chairman of the committee.

"During your whole examination there has not been a direct answer given to a question." "I wish to say to you," said the chairman, "that such equivocation is unworthy of you."

The plea needs no answer, but if it did, the language of the railroad men themselves supplies one that cannot be bettered. To the representatives of the people, who had telegraphed them for information "at once, as the excitement is intense, and we fear violence and destruction of property," General Mc-Clellan, of the Atlantic and Great Western, replied that the contract was "cancelled"; President Clark, of the Lake Shore, that it was "formally abrogated and cancelled"; Chairman Homer Ramsdell, of the Erie, that it was "abrogated"; Vice-president Thomas Scott, of the Pennsylvania Railroad, that it was "terminated officially"; Vice-president Vanderbilt, of the New York Central and Hudson River Railroad, that it was "cancelled with all the railroads."

Contracts that were not complete and in force would not need to be "cancelled" and "abrogated" and "terminated." These announcements were backed up by a telegram from the future head of the oil trust then incubating, in which he said of his company: "This company holds no contracts with the railroad companies." But in 1879 its secretary, called upon by the Ohio Legislature to produce the contracts the company had with the railroads, showed, among others, one covering the very date of this denial in 1872.

Before Congress the South Improvement Company sought to shelter themselves behind the plea that "their calculation was to get all the refineries in the country into the company. There was no difference made, as far as we were concerned, in favor of or against any refinery; they were all to come in alike."

How they "were all to be taken in" the contract itself showed. It bound the South Improvement Company "to expend large sums of money in the purchase of works for refining," and one of the reasons given by the railroads for making the contract was "to encourage the outlay." Upon what footing buyer and seller would meet in these purchases when the buyer had a secret arrangement like this with the owners of the sole way to and from wells, refineries, and markets, one does not need to be "a business man" to see. The would-be owners had a power to pry the property of the real owners out of their hands.

One of the Cleveland manufacturers who had sold was asked why he did so by the New York Legislature. They had been very prosperous, he said; their profits had been $30,000 to $45,000 a year; but their prosperity had come to a sudden stop.

"From the time that it was well understood in the trade that the South Improvement Company had . . . grappled the entire transportation of oil from the West to the seaboard . . . we were all kind of paralyzed, perfectly paralyzed; we could not operate. . . . The South Improvement Company, or some one representing them, had a drawback of a dollar, sometimes seventy cents, sometimes more, sometimes less, and we were working against that difference."

It was a difference, he said, which destroyed their business.

He went to the officials of the Erie and of the New York Central to try to get freight rates that would permit him to continue in business. "I got no satisfaction at all," he said; "I am too good a friend of yours," said the representative of the New York Central, "to advise you to have anything further to do with this oil trade."

"Do you pretend that you won't carry for me at as cheap a rate as you will carry for anybody else?"

"I am but human," the freight agent replied.

He saw the man who was then busily organizing the South Improvement Company. He was non-committal. "I got no satisfaction, except 'You better sell, you better get clear.' Kind of *sub rosa:* 'Better sell out, no help for it.'"

His firm was outside the charmed circle, and had to choose between selling and dying. Last of all, he had an interview with the president of the all-conquering oil company, in relation to the purchase of their works. "He was the only party that would buy. He offered me fifty cents on the dollar, on the construction account, and we sold out. . . . He made this expression, I remember: 'I have ways of making money that you know nothing of.'"

For the works, which were producing $30,000 to $45,000 a year profit, and which they considered worth $150,000, they received $65,000.

"Did you ascertain in the trade," he was asked, "what was the average rate that was paid for refineries?"

"That was about the figure. . . . Fifty cents on the dollar."

"It was that or nothing, was it not?"

"That or nothing."

The freight rates had been raised in February. This sale followed in three weeks.

"I would not have sold out," he told the Legislature, "if I could have got a fair show with the railways. My business, instead of being an enterprise to buy and sell, became degraded into running after the railways and getting an equal chance with others."

"The only party that would buy" gave his explanation a few years later of the centralization of this business.

"Some time in the year 1872," he swore, "when the refining business of the city of Cleveland was in the hands of a number of small refiners, and was unproductive of profit, it was deemed advisable by many of the persons engaged therein, for the sake of economy, to concentrate the business, and associate their joint capital therein. The state of the business was such at that time that it could not be retained profitably at the city of Cleveland, by reason of the fact that points nearer the oil regions were enjoying privileges not shared by refiners at Cleveland, and could produce refined oil at a much less rate than could be done at this point. It was a well-understood fact at that time among refiners that some arrangement would have to be made to economize and concentrate the business, or ruinous losses would not only occur to the refiners themselves, but ultimately Cleveland, as a point of refining oil, would have to be abandoned. At that time those most prominently engaged in the business here consulted together, and as a result thereof several of the refiners conveyed" to his company, then as always the centre of the centralization, "their refineries, and had the option, in pay therefor, to take stock" in this company, "at par, or to take cash." This company, he continued, "had no agency in creating this state of things which made that change in the refining business necessary at that time, but the same was the natural result of the trade, nor did it in the negotiations which followed use any undue or unfair means, but in all cases, to the general satisfaction of those whose refineries were acquired, the full value thereof, either in stock or cash, was paid as the parties preferred."

The producers were not to fare any better than the refiners. The president of the South Improvement Company said to a representative of the oil regions substantially: "We want you producers to make out a correct statement of the average production of each well, and the exact cost per barrel to produce the oil. Then we propose to allow you a fair price for the oil."

Within forty-eight hours after the freight rates were raised, according to the programme, "the entire business of the oil regions," the Titusville *Herald*, March 20, 1872, reported, "became paralyzed. Oil went down to a point seventy cents below the cost of production. The boring of new wells is suspended, existing wells were shut down. The business in Cleveland stopped almost altogether. Thousands of men were thrown out of work."

The people rose. Their uprising and its justification were described to the Pennsylvania Constitutional Convention of 1873 by a brilliant "anti-monopolist," "a rising lawyer" of Franklin, Venango Co. The principal subject to which he called the attention of his fellow-members was the South Improvement Company, and the light it threw on the problems of livelihood and liberty. Quoting the decision of the Pennsylvania Supreme Court in the Sanford case, he said:

That is the law in Pennsylvania to-day. But in spite of this decision, and in spite of the law, we well know that almost every railroad in this State has been in the habit, and is to-day in the habit, of granting special privileges to individuals, to companies in which the directors of such railroads are interested, to particular business, and to particular localities. We well know that it is their habit to break down certain localities, and build up others, to break down certain men in business and to build up others, to monopolize certain business themselves by means of the numerous corporations which they own and control, and all this in spite of the law, in defiance of the law.

The South Improvement Company's scheme would give that corporation the monopoly of the entire oil business of this State, amounting to $20,000,000 a year. That corporation was created by the Pennsylvania Legislature along with at least twenty others, under the name of improvement companies, within a few years past, all of which corporations contain the names as original corporators of men who may be found in and about the office of the Pennsylvania Railroad Company, in Philadelphia, when not lobbying at Harrisburg. The railroads took but one of those charters which they got from the Legislature, and by means of that struck a deadly blow at one of the greatest interests of the State. Their scheme was contrary to law, but before the legal remedy could have been applied, the oil business would have lain prostrate at their feet, had it not been prevented by an uprising of the people, by the threatenings of a mob, if you please, by threatening to destroy property, and by actually commencing to destroy the property of the railroad company, and had the companies not cancelled the contract which Scott and Vanderbilt and others had entered into, I venture to say there would not have been one mile of railroad track left in the County of Venango — the people had come to that pitch of desperation. . . . Unless we can give the people a remedy for this evil of discriminations in freight, they will sooner or later take the remedy into their own hands.

Soon after this attorney for the people was promoted from the poor pay of patriotism to a salary equal to that of the President of the United States, and to the place of counsel for the principal members of the combination, whose inwardness he had descried with such hawk-eye powers of vision. Later, as their counsel, he drafted the famous trust agreement of 1882.

The South Improvement Company was formed January 2d [1872]. The agreement with the railroads was evidently already worked out in its principal details, for the complicated contracts were formally signed, sealed, and delivered January 18th. The agreed increase of freights went into effect February 26th. The pacific insurrection of the people began with an impromptu mass-meeting at Titusville the next day, February 27th. Influential delegations, or committees, on transportation, legislation, conference with press, pipe lines, arresting of drilling, etc., were set to work by the organization thus spontaneously formed by the people. A complete embargo was placed on sales of oil at any price to the men who had made the hateful bargain with the railroads. The oil country was divided into sixteen districts, in each of which the producers elected a local committee, and over all these was an executive committee composed of representatives from the local committees — one from each. No oil was sold to be used within any district except to those buyers whom the local committee recommended; no oil was sold to be exported or refined outside the district, except to such buyers as the executive committee permitted. One cent a barrel was paid by each producer into a general fund for the expenses of the organization.

Steps were taken to form a company with a capital of $1,000,000, subscribed by the producers, to advance money, on the security of their oil, to those producers who did not want to sell.

Able lawyers were employed and sent with the committees to all the important capitals — Harrisburg, Washington, the offices of the railway companies. The flow of oil was checked, the activities of the oil world brought near a stop.

Monday, March 15th [1872], by the influence of the Washington committee, a resolution was introduced into the House of Representatives by Representative Scofield, ordering an investigation of the South Improvement Company. Immediately upon this the frightened participants cancelled the contracts. By the 26th of March the representatives of the people had secured a pledge in writing from the five great railroads concerned of "perfect equality," and "no rebates, drawbacks, or other arrangements," in favor of any one thereafter. March 30th, Congress began the investigation which brought to light the evidence of the contracts, and meanwhile the committees on legislation and pipe lines were securing from the Pennsylvania Legislature the repeal of the South Improvement Company charter, and the passage of a "so-called" Free Pipe Line law, discovered afterwards to be worthless on account of amendments shrewdly inserted by the enemy.

The committee of Congress noticed when the contracts were afterwards shown to it, that though they had been so widely declared to be "cancelled," they had not been cancelled, but were as fresh — seals, stamps, signatures and all — as the day they were made. This little circumstance is descriptive of the whole proceeding. Both parties to this scheme to give the use of the highways as a privilege to a few, and through this privilege to make the pursuit of livelihood a privilege, theirs exclusively — the railroad officials on one side, and their beneficiaries of the South Improvement Company on the other — were resolute in their determination to carry out their purpose. All that follows of this story is but the recital of the sleuthlike tenacity with which this trail of fabulous wealth has been followed.

The chorus of cancellation from the railroads came from those who had meant never to cancel, really. In their negotiations with the representatives of the people they had contested to the last the abandonment of the scheme. "Their friendliness" to it "was so apparent," the Committee of the Producers reported, "that we could expect little consideration at their hands," and the committee became satisfied that the railroads had made a new contract among themselves like that of the South Improvement Company, and to take its place. Its head frankly avowed before the Investigating Committee of Congress their intention of going ahead with the plan. "They are all convinced that, sooner or later, it will be necessary to organize upon the basis on which the South Improvement Company was organized, including both producers and refiners."

This conviction has been faithfully lived up to. Under the name of the South Improvement Company the arrangement was ostentatiously abandoned, because to persist in it meant civil war in the oil country as the rising young anti-monopolist lawyer pointed out in the Constitutional Convention. Mark Twain, in describing the labors of the missionaries in the Sandwich Islands, says they were so successful that the vices of the natives no longer exist in name — only in reality. As every page will show, this contract no longer exists in name — only in reality. In the oil world, and in every other important department of our industrial life — in food, fuel, shelter, clothing, transportation, this contract, in its various new shapes, has been kept steadily at work gerrymandering the livelihoods of the people.

The men who had organized the South Improvement Company paid the public revolt the deference of denial, though not of desistance. The company had got a charter, organized under it, collected twenty per cent. of the subscription for stock, made contracts with the railroads, held meetings of the directors, who approved of the contracts and had received the benefits of the increase of freights made in pursuance of the agreement. This was shown by the testimony of its own officers.

But "the company never did a dollar's worth of business," the Secretary of the Light of the World told Congress, and "there was never the slightest connection between the South Improvement Company and the Standard Oil Company," the president of the latter and the principal member of both [Rockefeller] said in an interview in the New York *World*, of March 29, 1890. "The South Improvement Company died in embryo. It was never completely organized, and never did any business. It was partly born, died, and was buried in 1872," etc.

Still later, before a committee of the Legislature of New York in 1888, he was asked about "the Southern Improvement Company."

"There was such a company?"

"I have heard of such a company."

"Were you not in it?"

"I was not."

"So help me God!"

At almost the moment of this denial in New York, an associate in this and all his other kindred enterprises, asked before Congress who made up the South Improvement Company, named as among them the principal members of the great oil company, and most conspicuous of them all was the name of this denier.

The efficiency with which this "partly born" innocent lived his little hour, "not doing a dollar's worth of business," was told in a summary phrase by one of the managers of the Pennsylvania Railroad, describing the condition of the oil business in 1873:

"All other of our largest customers had failed."

When the people of the oil regions made peace after their uprising it was, as they say, with "full assurance from the Washington committee that the throwing off the restrictions from trade will not embarrass their investigation (by

Congress), but that the Sub-Committee of Commerce will, nevertheless, continue, as the principle involved, and not this particular case alone, is the object of the investigation."

The Committee of Commerce did not "continue." The principal witness, who had negotiated the contracts by which the railroads gave over the business of the oil regions to a few, refused in effect, beyond producing copies of the contract, to be a witness. Permission was given by the Committee of Congress during its first zeal to the Committee of Producers from Pennsylvania to copy the testimony as it was taken, but no official record of its discoveries exists. This transcript was published by the producers, and copies are possessed by a few fortunate collectors. The committee did not report, and in the archives of the national Capitol no scrap of the evidence taken is to be found. All has vanished into the bottomless darkness in which the monopoly of light loves to dwell.

Allan Nevins: THE SOUTH IMPROVEMENT COMPANY — A QUEST FOR STABILITY

Lloyd's attack is rebutted here in a telling selection from the work of Allan Nevins (1890–   ). A leading American historian for almost 40 years who came to the field after a successful editorial career on major New York city newspapers, Professor Nevins has been astonishingly productive. He taught for thirty years at Columbia and continues to study and write at the Huntington Library in California. His distinction as a historian of the United States has won him many honors, including two Pulitzer Prizes and a Bancroft Prize, and many degrees. Nevins rejects Lloyd's assumption that the oil industry was in a prosperous and stable condition before Rockefeller planned his scheme. He sees the South Improvement Company (first suggested by railroad interests) as a defensive alliance of Cleveland refiners, joined hesitantly by Rockefeller, to meet bitter competition from the "Oil Regions" of Pennsylvania. In a later section of his biography of Rockefeller, however, Professor Nevins indicates his own view that the bitterness of the competition at the time did not fully justify the rebate system demanded by Standard Oil.

CHEAP transportation was vital to the oil trade, and rival refining centers worried ceaselessly over their railroad rates and facilities. Hence it was that when, in May, 1871, the Pennsylvania Railroad effected a 999-year lease of the United Canal and Railroad Companies in New Jersey, making New York its eastern terminus, startling rumors circulated among the Western oil men. The Penn-

Excerpted and reprinted with the permission of Charles Scribner's Sons from pages 95–105 of *Study in Power, John D. Rockefeller,* Volume I by Allan Nevins. Copyright 1953 Charles Scribner's Sons.

sylvania, ran one report, was offering fabulous rebates on crude oil shipments to the Long Island refiners, thus empowering the New Yorkers to undersell their Cleveland rivals. Thomas A. Scott intended to build a great freight business in oil between the regions and the seaboard cities; he would shoulder Cleveland and Pittsburgh roughly aside.

Cleveland had heard of comparable threats for years. "Fortunately for us," remarked the *Leader*, "the Erie managers have a keen eye on Mr. Scott, and we may rely upon them so to adapt their oil rates to the market that Cleveland refining interests will not seriously suffer." Pittsburgh meanwhile was heartened by the opening (June, 1871) of through traffic to Baltimore over the newly-completed Connellsville branch of the Baltimore & Ohio. Here, Pittsburghers believed, was an avenue of escape from the tyranny of the Pennsylvania, and they eagerly conferred with President Garrett of the B. & O. upon oil shipments to the coast. Pittsburgh and Regions oil interests were also encouraged by the strong movement of 1870–72 for a free pipe line bill; that is, granting pipe lines the right of eminent domain. If passed, this would make possible the pumping of crude oil from the Regions directly to Pittsburgh refineries, a far cheaper service than rail or river. In 1870 railroad interests crushed the bill in the State Senate after it passed the House; but the spring of 1871 found formidable delegations in Harrisburg to support it, and men hoped for eventual victory.

Thus the battle between rival railroads and their respective refining centers continued. Rockefeller watched its progress, but he had now come to feel that such rivalry was of secondary importance. What any group of manufacturers could do to another was in his opinion of far less consequence than what the depression might do to all of them.

For times had grown worse as 1871 neared its end. A writer in the Titusville *Herald* on November 8 estimated that "at present rates the loss to the refiner, on the average, is seventy-five cents per barrel." He called for an organization to stop "the spasmodic fluctuation in prices and ruinous shutting down of large and expensive works." Voices from Pittsburgh, Cleveland, and New York were quite as alarmed. The Pittsburgh *Commercial* on January 13, 1872, declared that "there has heretofore existed a ruinous competition between refineries, by which all parties have lost money. The entire petroleum business has been a losing one for the past year, not only for refiners and producers, but for the railroad companies who have transported the oil, the only parties who have profited by the situation being the foreign consumers."

Rockefeller long remembered this menacing period. In 1888 he wrote to S. C. T. Dodd that he and his brother Frank, reviewing the situation of 1871, had agreed that "more than three-fourths of the oil refiners of the country did a losing business that year." One prominent Clevelander, Alexander of Alexander, Scofield & Co., had offered his interest in his firm to Frank for ten cents on the dollar. After a lapse of fifty years, in 1921, Rockefeller still recalled vividly the dropping prices, the vanishing margin of profit, the sickening fluctuations and dark uncertainty. "A panic had been on for a considerable time in the oil refining business," he told W. O. Inglis, "resulting in loss to nearly all refiners." Most of his rivals had faced "impending ruin." The situation moved him to seek earnestly for a remedy, for he did not believe that the Standard Oil Company, despite its prosperous record, dared to let the existing situation continue.

Why this foreboding? According to orthodox economic theory, the situation was perfectly natural, and the overbalanced industry would soon right itself. Free competition was forcing prices below the cost of production. When they reached such a point, the most inefficient manufacturers would theoretically become discouraged and suspend operations. Supplies would then be reduced and prices would rise. While this process caused a great deal of human suffering, according to Manchester doctrine it made for enterprise, efficiency, and the welfare of the greatest number.

But Rockefeller knew that the theory no longer corresponded with realities, for it cost many units more to discontinue than to keep running. When competition drove prices below production costs, the big firms could not resort to a temporary shutdown. Their overhead, their interest on investment, their charges for maintenance automatically continued. These were heavy costs; to avoid bankruptcy the big establishment was forced to carry on even at a loss, selling at low prices to cover *part* of its expenses. It might be forced to do so for years, and come to bankruptcy after all. Thousands would be ruined, tens of thousands thrown out of work. Then the whole cycle would perhaps repeat itself.

Rockefeller felt that such a destructive process must be prevented. By combination, the big establishments could prevent a ruinous imbalance between manufacturing capacity and market demand, with excess productive facilities a heavy deadweight on the economy of the industry. They could also achieve manifold economies. "We recognized," he testified in the Federal anti-trust suit long afterward, "that if we would succeed we must,

if possible, increase the volume of our business with a given expense, and thus reduce the cost of the business in every department of manufacture and merchandizing."

The Standard Oil Company was the strongest in America, the most likely to survive a depression. Rockefeller had no anxiety for his personal future, for his holdings were varied and considerable. "You know we are independently rich outside of investments in oil," he wrote his wife in 1872. Yet he was convinced that he could not let the industry as a whole drift into deeper chaos. Some plan for unification and consequent control must be devised. In his hard-headed, far-seeing fashion, he discussed various possibilities with his partners. Meanwhile other men were also searching for a way out. The result was the emergence of two plans, the first that of a Pennsylvania group, the second that of Rockefeller and Flagler.

The idea of organizing to check overproduction and ruthless competition was not new in the oil industry. As early as the fall of 1866 producers in the Regions had discussed a combination "for the purpose of attempting to make better terms with the refiners in the price of the crude market." A year later the oil jobbers talked of launching a million-dollar Oil Buyers' Association. In 1868–69 came the league of Oil Regions refiners that boasted it would wipe Cleveland out as with a sponge. . . .

Rockefeller's distrust of the Oil Regions men was almost as strong as his fear of uncontrolled competition. What if the producers formed a really effective alliance with Regions refiners, perhaps including New York as well? As late as 1917 his resentful apprehensions of 1870 were still fresh in his mind. "Was not the Pennsylvania Railroad, with its ally, the

Empire Transportation Company, trying to eliminate Cleveland as a refining center, and did not the Oil City and Titusville papers boast that this could be done?"

Such distrust intensified his desire for combination, for he saw that some attempt to achieve it was inevitable — and should not this be made from Cleveland rather than from Philadelphia or New York? The Standard, shipping more than 3000 barrels of oil a day — fifty or sixty carloads — was the greatest refining organization in the world, and could exert tremendous force. As Rockefeller discussed the matter with Flagler, his ideas crystallized. His observation of the facts of any business situation was always searching, his deductions penetrating; and he soon made up his mind as to the necessary solution.

The carriers took rapid steps to acquire the greater part of the anthracite field by purchasing mines and coal acreage, a course which was legal in Pennsylvania at the time. Most of the few independent operators who survived were induced to sign long-term contracts with the roads for the carriage of their coal. In this fashion, by the end of 1871, seven great corporations almost completely controlled the anthracite supply: the five railroads named above, and two coal companies. Production was now adjusted to public demand, and freight rates were fixed by informal agreement among the roads. In 1873 they went a step further, and defying popular resentment, formed a pool to make their control of prices and freight rates complete.

The managers of the oil-carrying roads, or some of them, saw in 1871 that their problem had a close resemblance to that which President Franklin B. Gowen of the Reading and President Asa Packer of the Lehigh had faced in the anthracite field. In both instances the fates of the producers and carriers were related. In both there had been furious overproduction, price-cutting, and chaos. Of course, the railroads could not buy up the expanding oil fields or the hundreds of refineries. They might, however, encourage some control of production, perhaps through the chief refiners, while at the same time they could effect an agreement on freight rates. They complained that these rates, already less than a cent per ton-mile, were far below costs; that the irregularity of shipments, now a flood and now a trickle, burdened them with excess employees and rolling stock; and that bad shipping practices cost them heavily in train fires and explosions.

It was these facts and possibilities, together with certain other elements, which led to the South Improvement Company. What were the other elements? One was the growth of the Pennsylvania Railroad. By 1871 its tracks ran from New York to Chicago, opening prospects which excited J. Edgar Thomson, its president, and his energetic second in command, Tom Scott. Scott in particular was restless and ambitious. Already president of the Union Pacific, and soon to be elected head of the Texas & Pacific, he had dreams which covered the vast West and the reviving South. Wendell Phillips caustically remarked that as he trailed his garments across the country, the members of twenty legislatures rustled like leaves in a winter's wind behind him. The Nation declared just after the acquisition of the New Jersey lines that the Pennsylvania "will hereafter be practically omnipotent in the legislatures of three states, and perhaps more." Scott had his virtues; he had performed notable services as Assistant Secretary of War 1861–62, he was a man of personal graciousness and kindliness, and he supported many philanthropic enterprises. But "Tom Scottism" had become a term for egregious ambition.

This called for the consolidation of nearly all oil-refining units into one great organization, which would eliminate excess capacity and stop price-cutting. Rockefeller was convinced that a mere association or even pool could not long hold together. But he felt that with the Standard as a nucleus, a powerful merger could be achieved. "The idea was mine," he said long afterward. "The idea was persisted in, too, in spite of the opposition of some who became faint-hearted at the magnitude of the undertaking, as it constantly assumed larger proportions." A huge coöperative federation!

As Rockefeller did not commit his plan to paper, no documentary evidence of its existence in 1871 exists. Some writers have therefore assumed that he had no plan prior to the organization of the South Improvement Company, soon to appear. But Rockefeller and Flagler always denied any part in devising this company. "It was not our idea," the former categorically told W. O. Inglis. "We had an idea of our own." He described how the formation of the Refiners' Association led him and Flagler to discuss the problem of "protecting the industry," and how out of their talks emerged his own project. "We were gathering information which confirmed us in the idea that to enlarge our own Standard Oil of Ohio and actually take into partners with us the refining interest would accomplish the protection of the oil industry as a whole." In the federal anti-trust suit he testified respecting the founders of the South Improvement Company: "We did not share their views as to the plan. We so frankly stated to them, and more than once."

. . . The origins of this scheme are of particular interest. By 1871 the railroads of the United States had done a good deal of experimenting with that form of combination called the pool. A group of roads serving the same district would agree to maintain rates at a fixed level, and divide the traffic or the revenues on a prearranged scale. In studying the difficult oil situation — and the frantic rate wars of 1870–71 had made railroad leaders study it furiously — the managers were much interested by recent events in the anthracite coal field.

Here during the Civil War profitable contracts and rising prices had brought about a hectic development of new mines. When peace came, a bitter competition for the suddenly limited market set in. Operators in the various districts slashed prices recklessly. Inevitably the five coal-carrying roads — the Reading, the Lehigh Valley, the Delaware & Hudson, the Lackawanna, and the New Jersey Central — were drawn into the conflict. When coal operators along the Lackawanna cut their prices sharply in 1867, the Lehigh Valley promptly reduced its freight rates to permit Lehigh mine owners to keep on competing. A continuance of price and rate slashing would have ruined operators and roads alike. But by 1871 a solution was being found.

At this very time the Pennsylvania legislature, one of the twenty, was responding to pressure from Scott and others by chartering a number of corporations with extraordinary powers. As yet the holding company had virtually no existence in America. Some states, New York and Ohio among them, even forbade one corporation to hold the stock of another. But in 1868–72 the legislators at Harrisburg, by special enactments, gave more than forty corporations amazing charters, with powers including the right to hold the stock of other companies in or out-side the state. One of them, the South Improvement Company, was chartered in the spring of 1870, with Tom Scott's private secretary and two of Scott's friends its incorporators. It was not cre-ated for any specific purpose, and was soon on sale to the highest bidder.

The promoters of the "new view" for controlling oil refining and transporta-tion quietly bought the charter, complet-ing the purchase January 2, 1872. They immediately sold a group of insiders 1100 shares at $100 a share 20 per cent thereon being paid into the treasury. And who were these promoters? The idea that Rockefeller and Flagler were among them is quite baseless. The plan was primarily a railroad project. Tom Scott stood sponsor in the background. . . . This evidence overthrows the old view that Rockefeller or Flagler was responsible for the enterprise. Actually, their subsequent denials were emphatic, and were never contradicted by those who knew the facts. Although they never apologized for their support of the scheme, they always asserted that their faith in it was limited. "We did not be-lieve in it," Flagler declared. Both felt that their own plan was the only one likely to succeed. "It was apparent to the leaders of the Standard Oil Company," said Rockefeller in a conversation long afterward, "that one common ownership, with the simple ideas which controlled the Standard Oil Company, was the only really feasible thing."

Why, then, did the South Improve-ment idea "begin to grow" on Rocke-feller that November night in New York? For one reason, the situation seemed desperate — refined oil in New York was selling at 22.33 cents a gallon, one of the lowest prices yet known. For another, a trial of the scheme seemed only good policy. Here were the Pennsylvania re-finers and two railroads bringing a co-öperative plan on a silver platter. Pos-sibly it would work. Whatever the event, to antagonize its promoters would be bad policy, for the Standard might want their aid in the future.

Rockefeller phrased his position crisply years later: "We acceded to it because he [Tom Scott] and the Philadelphia and Pittsburgh men, we hoped, would be helpful to us ultimately. We were will-ing to go with them as far as the plan could be used; so that when it failed, we would be in a position to say, 'Now try our plan.' Thus we would be in a much better position to get their coöperation than if we had said 'No' from the start."

An outline of the scheme will make clear both its strength and weakness. It was essentially a plan to unite the oil-carrying railroads in a pool; to unite the refiners in an association, the South Im-provement Company; and to tie the two elements together by agreements which would stop destructive price-cutting and restore freight charges to a profitable level. The railroads were to divide the oil freights on a prearranged scale; the refiners were to act as *eveners*, insuring each road its quota of business; and in return the refiners were to get rate con-cessions which would wipe out all recal-citrant competitors. The authors had a hazy notion of bringing the producers into the combination. They said later that had their company not been ready-named, they would have called it "The American Cooperative Refining Com-pany."

Committee on Manufactures: A TRUST IS FORMED

*In 1889 the Committee on Manufactures of the House of Repre-
sentatives reported back on its investigation of certain trusts. During
the early testimony on the Sugar Trust, the original Deed of Incorporation of that trust was submitted in evidence before the Committee.
The deed is an important historical document, and like all such documents must be read with care, so as not to read in too much or too little
either along or between the lines.*

DEED

The Sugar Refineries' Company

THE undersigned, namely: Have-
meyers & Elder, The Decastro and
Donner Sugar Refining Company, F. O.
Matthiessen and Weichers Sugar Refin-
ing Company, Havemeyer Sugar Refin-
ing Company, Brooklyn Sugar Refining
Company, the firm of Dick & Meyer, the
firm of Moller, Sierck & Co., North River
Sugar Refining Company, the firm of
Oxnard Brothers, The Standard Sugar
Refinery, The Bay State Sugar Refinery,
The Boston Sugar Refining Company,
The Continental Sugar Refinery, and
The Revere Sugar Refinery, for the pur-
pose of forming the board hereinafter
provided for, and for the other purposes
hereinafter set forth, enter into the following agreement:

NAME

The board herein provided for shall be
designated by the name of The Sugar
Refineries' Company.

OBJECTS

The objects of this agreement are:

1. To promote economy of administration and to reduce the cost of refining,
thus enabling the price of sugar to be
kept as low as is consistent with reasonable profit.

2. To give to each refinery the benefit
of all appliances and processes known or
used by the others, and useful to improve
the quality and diminish the cost of refined sugar.

3. To furnish protection against unlawful combinations of labor.

4. To protect against inducements to
lower the standard of refined sugars.

5. Generally to promote the interests
of the parties hereto in all lawful and
suitable ways.

BOARD

The parties hereto who are not corporations shall become such before this
deed takes effect.

Each corporation subscribing hereto
agrees, and the parties hereto who are
not corporations agree as to the corporations which they are to form, that all the
shares of the capital stock of all such cor-

From the House of Representatives, Committee on Manufactures, "Report in Relation to the Sugar
Trust and Standard Oil Trust," 50th Congress, 1st Session (Washington, D. C., 1889), Government
Printing Office.

porations shall be transferred to a board, consisting of eleven persons, which may be increased to thirteen by vote of a majority of the members of the entire board, the two additional members to belong respectively to the first and second classes hereinafter provided for.

Any member of the board may be removed by vote of two-thirds of the members of the entire board in case of incapacity or neglect or refusal to serve.

Any member may resign by filing written notice of his resignation with the secretary of said board.

Vacancies during the term of office of members shall be filled by appointment by vote of the majority of the members of the entire board.

A member appointed to fill a vacancy shall hold office until the expiration of the term of the member in whose place he is appointed, which new appointee shall succeed to all the rights, duties, and obligations of his predecessor under this deed.

Vacancies by expiration of office shall be filled at the annual meeting of the holders of certificates herein provided for, or at such other times as shall be prescribed by the board.

Such annual meetings shall be held in the city of New York, in the month of June, and notice shall be given to each certificate holder of record of every meeting of certificate holders, by mailing to him, at least seven days before said meeting, a notice of the time, place, and objects of such meeting. Holders of certificates shall vote according to the number of shares for which they hold certificates. They may vote by proxy.

The board may make by-laws. All arrangements for meetings, elections, and all details not herein specifically provided for, shall be made by the board. A member of the board may act by proxy for any other member with like effect as if he were present and acting.

A majority of the members of the board shall constitute a quorum for the transaction of business. The action of a board meeting, by a majority vote of such meeting, shall have the same effect as the unanimous action of the board, except as herein otherwise provided, and that to authorize the appropriation of money, bonds, or shares, shall require the assent, either written or expressed, by vote at a board meeting, of at least a majority of the members of the entire board.

No member of the board shall, during the time that he holds office, buy or sell sugar or be interested directly or indirectly in the purchase or sale of sugar, whether for the purpose of speculation or otherwise, without a vote of a majority of the members of the entire board. For any violation of this provision he may be removed as a member of the board and shall be liable to account for all profits which shall be realized by him to the board for the pro rata benefit of the certificate holders.

As it is desirable that the board shall consist of members who are largely interested in the properties and the business contemplated, it is hereby agreed that all members of the board shall be free to join in or become parties to agreements and transactions which the several boards of directors hereinafter referred to, or this board, may arrange, to the same extent and in the same manner and with the like effect as if they were not members of the board. . . .

OFFICERS

The board shall appoint from its members a president, vice-president, and treasurer, and it shall also appoint a secretary, who may or may not be a member of the board. The board may from time to time create other offices and appoint the persons to fill them. It may appoint committees. It shall designate the duties and prescribe the powers of the several officers and committees.

PLAN

The several corporations, parties to this agreement, shall maintain their separate organizations and each shall carry on and conduct its own business.

The capital stock of each corporation shall be transferred to the board, and in lieu of the same certificates not exceeding $50,000,000, divided into 500,000 shares, each of $100, shall be issued by the board and distributed as hereinafter provided. . . .

The shares of the capital stock of the several corporations to be transferred to the board as herein provided shall be transferred to the names of the board as trustees, to be held by them and by their successors as members of the board strictly as joint tenants.

By the death, resignation, or removal of any member of the board, the whole title shall remain in the others. All members ceasing to be such shall execute such instrument as may be necessary, if any, to keep the title vested in the persons who from time to time shall be members of the board.

The board shall hold the stock transferred to it with all the rights and powers incident to stockholders in the several corporations and subject only to the purposes set forth in this deed. . . .

In consideration of the transfer of their stock to the board, the board shall also pay to Havemeyers & Elder the sum of * , to the F. O. Matthiessen and Weichers Sugar Refining Company the sum of * , and to the Bay State Sugar Refining Company the sum of * on account of

payments already made on pending contracts for improvements and enlargements.[1]

Additional shares to the amount of $400,000, less 15 per cent. to be left with the board as hereinafter provided, shall be received by Moller, Sierck & Co. for improvements and enlargement of capacity of their refinery now in progress, when said improvements are completed and the increased capacity demonstrated.

The shares assigned to the several refineries shall be distributed by them to and among the parties interested therein.

Each holder of stock in a refinery company shall be entitled to so many of the shares allotted to such refinery as shall be in proportion of his stock to the capital of his company.

Shares for stockholders of any refining company who shall not surrender their stock, may, under the direction of the board, be deposited for their account with the right to receive the same upon the surrender of their stock.

Of the shares allotted to the several refineries they shall leave 15 per cent. with the board, and these shares and any shares not allotted of the $50,000,000, except as herein otherwise provided, shall be subject to be disposed of by the board either for the acquisition of other refineries, to become parties to this deed, payment for additional capacity, or by appropriations to the several refineries.

But in no case shall any appropriation be made to or any action be taken by any corporation without the approval of its board of directors, and no action be taken by the board which shall create liability by it or by its members.

PROFITS

The profits arising from the business

---

[1] The Sugar Trust declined to reveal these amounts to the Committee.

of each corporation shall be paid over by it to the board hereby created, and the aggregate of said profits, or such amount as may be designated for dividends, shall be proportionately distributed by said board, at such time as it may determine, to the holders of the certificates issued by said board for capital stock, as hereinbefore provided.

FISCAL ARRANGEMENTS

The funds necessary to enable the said board to make the payments herein provided to be made by it may be raised by mortgage to be made by the corporations, or either, any, or all of them, on their property, and by such other means as shall be satisfactory to such board.

In case any mortgage shall be laid on the property of any corporation by its directors or stockholders, the holders of certificates shall, within a time to be fixed by said board, have the right, at such uniform rates as said board shall arrange, to have the bonds, certificates, or other evidence of debt or interest in proportion to their respective holdings. Any parts which shall not be thus taken may be disposed of by said board.

CHANGES

The number of shares and the total amount thereof issuable by said board may from time to time be increased or diminished by deed executed by a majority in value of the certificate holders.

The provisions of this deed may from time to time be changed by deed executed by not less than a majority in interest of the certificate holders, provided no change shall be made which shall discriminate to the disadvantage of the certificate holders as between themselves.

ACQUISITION OF OTHER REFINERIES

The capital stock of other sugar-refining companies and of companies whose business relates directly or indirectly to sugar refining (in every instance to be incorporated) may be transferred to said board with the consent of a majority thereof at valuation and upon terms satisfactory to it, to be held by said board under and subject to all the terms of this deed, and certificates may be issued therefor by said board, and may be sold by it to provide funds for such purchase or purchases, and any such corporation or corporations shall thereupon become a party to this deed upon causing the same to be duly signed in its behalf.

CUSTODY OF DEED

This deed, when executed by the parties hereto, shall be delivered to the president of the board, who shall have the sole and independent custody and control of the same, and the said deed shall not be shown or delivered to any corporation, firm, person, or persons whatsoever, except by the express direction and order of the board.

A copy of said deed shall be also lodged with a member of the board residing in Boston, Mass., which shall be held by him under the same condition and in the same manner as the original deed.

In witness whereof the parties have hereto set their seals and affixed their names, these presents to become binding when completely executed by all the parties, and to take effect from October 1, 1887.

Dated August 16, 1887.

HAVEMEYERS & ELDER.

DONNER & DE CASTRO SUGAR REFG. Co., per H. O. HAVEMEYER, *Manager.* (Subject to confirmation stock and scrip holders.)

F. O. MATTHIESSEN & WEICHERS SUGAR REFG. Co., F. O. MATTHIESSEN, *P.*

HAVEMEYER SUGAR REFINING COM-
PANY, JNO. E. SEARLES, JR., *Treasr.*
DICK & MEYER.
NORTH RIVER SUGAR REFINING CO.,
GEO. H. MOLLER, *Secretary.*
OXNARD BROS.
MOLLER, SIERCK & CO.
BROOKLYN SUGAR REFINING CO., HENRY
OFFERMAN, *Treas.*
STANDARD SUGAR REFINING CO., by
CHARLES O. FOSTER, *Pres.*
BAY STATE SUGAR REFG. CO., per ED-
WIN F. ATKINS, *Prest.*
CONTINENTAL SUGAR REFINERY, by SI-
LAS PIREE, *President.*

The undersigned hereby agree to be-

come parties to the foregoing deed in
accordance with the terms and conditions therein stated, they to receive without discount the amounts in certificates
set opposite their respective signatures:

FOREST CITY SUGAR REFINING CO., by
H. J. LIBBY, *President;* GEO. S.
HUNT, *Treas.*
ST. LOUIS SUGAR REFINING CO., by
W. L. NOOTT, *President;* A. D. CUN-
NINGHAM, *Sect. and Treasurer.*
PLANTERS' SUGAR REFINING CO. NEW
ORLEANS, JOHN BARKLEY, *Prest.*
LOUISIANA SUGAR REFINING CO., JOHN
S. WALLIS, *President.*

United States Industrial Commission: SUGAR REFINERS STRUGGLE TO SURVIVE

Under the authority of a federal act of 1898 the United States Indus-
trial Commission was created to investigate the national economy.
The Commission was made up of members from both houses of Con-
gress and nine presidential nominees, and it also made extensive use
of leading contemporary economic experts. The Industrial Commis-
sion's Report, published in 19 volumes between 1900 and 1902, is an
unusual source for students of American economic history. Four vol-
umes [I, II, XIII, and XVIII (Europe)] are concerned with trusts.
The extract which follows comes from the summary of testimony on
the Sugar Trust given in Volume I. In it we see testimony which is
sometimes frank in explanation and sometimes defensive. The extract
is rich in factual detail and in contemporary opinions, as leading sugar
refiners speak out on the question of the bitter price war, the rebate
system, and the struggle to survive through combination.

CAUSES OF ORGANIZATION

A. *Excessive competition* — Prior to the
formation of the Sugar Trust in 1887,
competition had become so excessive
that prices were reduced to an unremu-

nerative figure. The margin between the
prices of raw and refined sugar was only
0.71 cent in 1884, 0.78 in 1885, and 0.76
in 1886. Eighteen out of about 40 refineries had failed.

From United States Industrial Commission: *Report on Trusts and Industrial Combinations,* Vol. 1,
Washington, D. C. (1900), Topical Digest of Evidence, pp. 59–65.

Mr. Atkins,[1] who sold his refinery to the American Sugar Refining Company in 1887, states that the refining of sugar in those days was not profitable. The refining capacity was largely in excess of the demand; everybody wanted to run full time, and the consequence was that none of the refiners made any money. His own company had been improving its plant for a number of years, but had paid no dividends.

B. *Undue protection by tariff* — Mr. Havemeyer[2] further implies, without a very direct statement, that the higher protection formerly afforded to the business of sugar refining was a contributory cause of the formation of the trust, although he considers the present protection insufficient. Under the former laws the profits were apparently so great that competition was unduly stimulated, and the combination was formed with a view to securing the possible advantages of the protection. It should be noted that Mr. Havemeyer specifically declares that the tariff is the prime cause of the formation of most combinations. The following is quoted from Mr. Havemeyer's testimony:

"Q. But I asked you this question: If the refining industry of this country was built up under protection or a free-trade system? — A. Protection; enormous protection. Without the tariff I doubt if we should have dared to take the risk of forming the trust. It could have been done; but I certainly should not have risked all I had, which was then embarked in the sugar business, in a trust unless the business had been protected *as it was* by the tariff."

[1] Edwin F. Atkins, former independent sugar refiner of Boston, who amalgamated with the Havemeyer trust.
[2] Henry O. Havemeyer, president of the American Sugar Refining Company.

"Q. I put those two things together — first that the protective system has brought such domestic competition that you are compelled to form a trust to keep each others' throats from being cut? — A. That is just the case with sugar. Have I not just told you that prior to the formation of the Sugar Trust 18 companies went out of business, failed, were ruined, and that is the advantage of the tariff? But if you do not stick to real protection in itself, but give these producers 40 to 60 per cent, then they are bent on mulcting the public. The great trouble is the tariff, and there you are."

EFFECT ON OUTPUT, PRICES, AND COMPETITION

A. *Control of output* — Mr. Havemeyer's testimony before the Lexow committee in 1896 was read to him, and he stated that he stood by every word of it. In that testimony he was asked as to his evidence before the United States Senate committee in 1894, wherein he said that the trust was organized "with a view of controlling the price and output to the people of this country." He answered that that object of combination was not in his mind now, though it doubtless was when he made the statement. He would rather say now that the intention was to control the output of the refineries joining the trust and the price of their products. "It goes without saying that a man who produces 80 per cent of an article can control the price by not producing." He admitted that his company undoubtedly, in fact, controlled the product and price in the United States. The formation of the trust removed competition to a great extent.

The present output of the American Sugar Refining Company, according to Mr. Havemeyer, is about 30,000 barrels a day, its capacity about 40,000 barrels.

The witness believes it is now producing 90 per cent of the total output and could produce 20 per cent more than the entire demand. The various competing refineries could probably produce 50 per cent of the required output. In 1896 the witness testified before the New York committee that his company produced from 75 to 80 per cent of the refined output. In 1891, when the trust was changed to a corporation, it was making 67 per cent of the entire product.

Mr. Post[3] is of the opinion that the American Sugar Refining Company does not restrict production abnormally. All business is regulated by supply and demand. The capacity of refineries exceeds consumption, so that there must be some restriction. If it were not for combination, failure of some refineries, owing to excessive competition, would soon close them as effectually as under combination. Competing refineries at present are operating on as small a scale as possible, because profits are little or nothing. The Mollenhauer and National refineries have probably averaged about one-third of their capacity during the first 6 months of 1899.

B. *Variations of prices according to competition* — 1. Generally — Testimony concerning the effect of the sugar combination on prices indicates that there have been great fluctuations in the margin between raw and refined sugars since the formation of the trust in 1887, owing to the establishment from time to time of competing refineries, some of which have later been absorbed by the combination. . . . Immediately after the formation of the trust in 1887 prices were raised considerably to offset the excessively low prices of the preceding years.

The margin in 1888 was 1.258 cents.

Mr. Thurber[4] adds that when the business was got into working order and economies in manufacture had been effected by closing inferior plants, this margin was reduced.

Mr. Havemeyer and Mr. Post merely call attention to the reductions in the margin caused by the competition of the Spreckels' refineries, which began in 1889, and the less severe competition of the Mollenhauer refinery, established in 1890. The margin stood at 0.7 cent in 1890 and 0.8 in 1891. In the latter part of 1891 the Spreckels' refineries were bought up, and the margin was raised to 1.1 cents, which, as Mr. Havemeyer states, "is the usual margin we had laid out as necessary for the benefit of the stockholders and proper conduct of the business." The removal of the tariff on refined sugar in 1890 is also stated to have affected the price, although its effect on the margin is not clearly pointed out. The National and McCahan refineries were established in 1892, but there seems to have been little competition until the establishment of the Arbuckle and Doscher refineries, in 1898. The "interlopers" have brought the margin below 0.5 cent, destroying all profit.

The history of the competition of these two last-named refineries is given more in detail by several witnesses.

2. Arbuckle Brothers — Mr. Jarvie,[5] a member of the firm, testifies that Arbuckle Brothers started a wholesale grocery in Pittsburg in 1858. They began business in New York in 1870, making a specialty of roasted coffee in pound packages. Having a patented method of filling, packing, and weighing, they

---

[3] James H. Post of Brooklyn, commission agent of the Mollenhauer and the National Sugar Refining Companies of New York.

[4] F. B. Thurber, merchant, and president of the United States Export Association.

[5] James N. Jarvie of New York, a partner of Arbuckle Brothers.

sought to apply it to handling sugar as well as coffee. They found it impossible to make money by buying sugar from refineries, and so established a refinery, which began operation in September, 1898. Its capacity is about 4,000 barrels daily, and the witness believes it can refine as cheaply as the American Sugar Refining Company. Before Arbuckle Brothers entered business the margin between raw and refined sugar was about 90 cents per 100 pounds. The American Sugar Refining Company began cutting prices, apparently with the purpose of crushing the Arbuckles out of business. The Arbuckles have followed the prices made by the American Company, unless they believed it was cutting secretly, when they made open cuts.

Arbuckle Brothers think that they can stand the losses if a company selling 90 per cent of the total product is losing on the entire amount, and they are in business to stay. Offers for purchase of their refinery have been made by outside parties, but there have been no conferences with the American Company directly. Arbuckle Brothers have markets in various parts of the country, depending on freight rates. They do not believe freight discriminations are made in favor of the American Company. The prices of both concerns are the same, but some dealers and consumers prefer Arbuckle sugar, which they consider superior. The American Company is putting up sugar in small cotton bags to compete with Arbuckle packages.

According to Mr. JARVIE, the present excessive competition has completely destroyed profits. The evils of excessive competition would be lessened "if the American Sugar Refining Company should be willing to sell less than 100 per cent of all the sugar sold in this country."

Mr. DOSCHER[6] also believes that the American Company has generally cut prices first and Arbuckle Brothers followed, their prices usually being the same. At one time in December, 1898, however, the Arbuckles cut one-sixteenth cent below the American. This was the lowest price reached. The margin necessary for profit is 50 to 60 cents, while the actual margin has been running between 32 and 51 cents.

An important incident of the competition between the American Sugar Refining Company and Arbuckle Brothers is that the former has entered the coffee business in retaliation, so as to compete with the Arbuckles in their own field.

Mr. HAVEMEYER testifies that the American Sugar Refining Company "are in the coffee business, and in it to stay." Havemeyer & Elder bought out the Woolson Spice Company, of Toledo, and sold it to the Sugar Company. The price of coffee has been greatly reduced by this competition. Previously the price of green coffee had been 10 cents, of roasted 15. The cost of roasting is about 3 cents. The Sugar Company reduced the margin to 2½ cents, the price of green coffee meanwhile having dropped to 6 cents because of the great increase in the crop. The Sugar Company desired to avoid excessive cutting of prices by making a superior quality of coffee. The first cut was made largely through the fear of a fall in the value of the stock on hand by the decline of the price of green coffee.

Mr. JARVIE confirms this evidence as to the course of prices of coffee. The American Sugar Refining Company, he adds, is selling roasted coffee for 8½ cents, made from a grade of green coffee costing about 6 cents. The Arbuckles' coffee is

[6] Claus Doscher of Brooklyn, independent sugar refiner.

sold for 9 cents, their green coffee being worth more than 6 cents. The former difference between green and roasted coffee was 5 cents, so that profits have been greatly reduced by the competition.

3. Doscher refinery — Mr. DOSCHER testifies that the New York Refining Company began operations November 1, 1898, the margin between raw and refined sugar having varied during that year from 79 to 97 cents. The American Sugar Refining Company was already cutting prices against the Arbuckles and the margin kept getting lower. It has varied between 32 and 51 cents. The American Company has usually cut prices first, the New York Company following, but at one time the latter followed a lower cut made by the Arbuckles, maintaining it for 7 days. The American Company has made some special cuts in localities where it had refineries near. The witness has heard and believes that officers of the American Company have expressed the intention of putting down prices sufficiently to run him out of business, and that they thereby hope to prevent others from competing for some years to come. But he never heard anyone state that he had heard this actually said by such officers. The witness has had no conferences with the American Company nor with the Arbuckle Company as to selling his property or for any other purpose. He has been questioned by outsiders as to whether his company wanted to sell, but does not know whom they represented. The witness formerly owned the Brooklyn refinery, which joined the trust, and he now owns stock in the American Company.

Mr. DOSCHER has been unable to earn any profit by refining with the present margin of about 50 cents per 100 pounds, but has made some gains by advances in prices of raw sugar on hand. The witness believes the cost of refining in his establishment as low as in any other, but does not know what it costs others, nor exactly what it will cost him when under more regular operation. He had expected to make a nice profit if the margin of from 70 to 97 cents had continued. The capacity of his refinery is about 1,000,000 pounds, or 3,000 barrels, per day.

4. Other refineries — Besides the Arbuckle and Doscher refineries there are several other smaller ones outside of the trust. The independent refineries are enumerated by Mr. HAVEMEYER as follows: Arbuckle, Doscher, Mollenhauer, and National, of New York, Nash & Spalding of Boston, McCahan of Philadelphia, Cunningham of Galveston, Henderson & Cogswell of New Orleans, and the Crockett Refinery of San Francisco; their capacity is equal to 50 per cent of the required output. In answer to the question whether the American Sugar Refining Company had any interest in the Mollenhauer and Nash refineries, the witness said: "I prefer not to state about that. That is a little bit too private."

Mr. POST, as selling agent of the Mollenhauer and National refineries, knows that they do not sell under agreement with the American Company, but are entirely independent. He knows also that the American Company does not control the Arbuckle, Doscher, Nash, McCahan, or California Beet Sugar and Refining companies, nor two or three in Louisiana and Texas. These refineries are now running much under their capacity, being willing to allow the American Company to sell most of sugar at existing prices. The witness believes the American Company will cease excessive cutting before long.

Mr. THURBER states that while the

Mollenhauer, Doscher, and Union refineries have no connection with the American Sugar Refining Company, they do not extensively cut prices in competition. They follow prices set by the trust, demand being sufficient to take their output, although it takes only about two-thirds of the capacity of the American Company. Sometimes refiners having a surplus stock temporarily cut prices.

A. *Policy of trust toward competitors* — The general policy of the American Sugar Refining Company toward its competitors is stated by Mr. HAVEMEYER in this way: It is very vital to the prosperity of the company to keep up its output. When competitors begin business, prices must be lowered with the primary purpose of retaining trade. If the result is to crush competitors, that is their affair, not the affair of the trust. It is thus the purpose of the trust to see to it that competitors do not stay in business too long. Moreover, it aims to keep prices so low that additional competition will not be likely to be provoked.

B. *General tendency of combination regarding prices* — Broad statements of opinion as to the general influence of the trust on prices and its effect on the consumer are made by several witnesses.

Thus Mr. THURBER believes that although prices were raised above the ruinous figures prevailing before the organization of the trust, reduction to reasonable figures followed as soon as savings in cost of production began to be made.

Mr. POST believes that the combination has reduced prices to consumers. The company has not used its possible power to secure exorbitant profits, but has kept the margin small because of existing and possible future competition. The witness believes the margin would have been greater if the trust had not

been formed, in spite of the fact that it was so low before it was organized. The weaker houses would have been driven out and demand for sugar would have exceeded the capacity of surviving refineries, forcing up prices. But if the American company had exclusive control, he adds, it would be dangerous. Its managers might not always be as broad minded as Mr. Havemeyer. Competing refineries do influence prices in the interest of consumers. But if the number of competing refineries were increased there would be no gain, for some would soon be driven out of business.

The same witness adds, in this connection, that the price of refined sugar does not always show the real sum received by refiners; often one-eighth cent should be deducted, owing to methods of selling. This would affect the margin similarly. The figures above quoted show the average margin from 1890 to 1898 to be 14 cents per 100 pounds less than for the 7 years before the organization of the trust in 1887. The average from 1888 to 1898 was 96.6; from 1885 to 1887, when competition had destroyed all profit, about 75.

Mr. ATKINS, whose refinery joined the American Sugar Refining Company at the time of its organization, testifies that the combination is manufacturing sugar at such a low cost that it would scarcely be possible to compete profitably against it. With the small amount of protection which now exists, the American refiner must economize in every way possible to undersell the European competitor. While it is possible that independent companies or an association of them may at some time effectively compete against the American Sugar Refining Company, it is scarcely probable. The witness believes that the price of sugar has been on the whole reduced to the people by the combination. The lower refined sugar is sold the larger the demand; consequently it is profitable to reduce the margin as far as possible.

Mr. HAVEMEYER states clearly the policy of the trust as to prices. He does not "care 2 cents for your ethics," but thinks it is fair and right as a business proposition "to get out of the consumer all you can," consistently with business principles. While a trust could perhaps demand the utmost prices that the consumer would bear, it is quite another matter whether it would do so. They would be kept as high as possible without provoking additional competition. In view of the economy of concentrated production, the witness believes that the trust could thus make proper profits, while the consumer would obtain goods at lower prices than before combination, and competitors with fewer economies would not be inclined to enter. When competitors do start in business, it is the policy of the sugar combination to secure the continuation of its output, which is very vital, and therefore to see to it that they do not stay in business too long.

Trusts are not in business for their health, nor will they sell their product for less than they can get unless for sufficient reason. Nevertheless, combinations in all articles would be beneficial to the consumer. The consumer benefits by the reduction of prices during the fight with competitors. If competitors are driven out the losses would be evened up by higher prices, but in the long run prices would be reasonable.

In the sugar business, Mr. Havemeyer adds, the competition of the Louisiana crop, lasting from about December 1 to March 1, tends regularly to depress prices and margin, after which the policy of the trust is to increase the margin so that the rate of average profit is about one-fourth cent per pound, which in the long run is the rate deemed most advantageous to the trust, in view of possible competition. The witness elsewhere refers to the desire of the trust to maintain a margin of about 1.1 cents between raw and refined sugar, as fair to the stockholders. The period up to 1893 is especially referred to in this connection.

C. Method of fixing prices – Mr. POST testifies that the prices are usually announced at the office of the American Company in the morning, and if other refiners change their prices that is announced a little later. Usually competitors follow the price fixed unless they have a surplus of sugar which they want to dispose of immediately, when they may keep the price one-sixteenth to one-eighth cent below the American Company. Preferences of grocers, and of brokers who distribute sugars to wholesale grocers, influence purchases where prices vary. The brokers of the Mollenhauer and National companies fix prices for their product, but after consultation with those companies.

D. Rebates – Several witnesses describe – their testimony agreeing in its general outlines – the system of rebates to wholesale grocers in the handling of sugar, and its effects. The system was introduced at the instance and for the advantage of the wholesalers, not of the trust itself. It has not been used largely as a means for controlling the trade by the combination.

Previous to the formation of the Wholesale Grocers' Association, about 1888, competition had completely wiped out all profits in handling sugar, which constituted a large proportion of the business of wholesale grocers. The association agreed to sell sugar at an advance of one-fourth cent per pound on its cost.

This arrangement was broken up, and certain leading jobbers then conferred with the American Sugar Refining Company. It was agreed that sugar should be billed to the wholesalers at three-sixteenths cent above the previous price, and that after 3 months a rebate of three-sixteenths cent per pound should be paid by the combination, provided sugar had not been sold at less than the price billed. This arrangement was agreed to by practically all dealers in New York, New Jersey, and New England, and it was later extended over the entire country. This rebate allowed grocers, probably, a small profit, estimated by Mr. Thurber at about 4 per cent, although Mr. Smith is doubtful whether there is any profit.

The following is the circular formerly employed by the American Sugar Refining Company in proposing to individual jobbers the terms of the rebate system.

New York, ——, 189 .

Dear Sir: We inclose herewith invoice of even date, from which you are entitled to our usual deductions of 1 per cent trade discount on 100-barrel lots and 1 per cent for cash if paid within 7 days.

Should you so desire, we shall be pleased, upon receipt of within written request, to constitute you one of our agents, in which case sugar will be consigned to you for sale as our factor, upon the following terms, the title to remain in us subject to your advances and return to you of your necessary outlay.

1. You are to advance to us within 30 days the amount of the invoice, which will be made up at our daily quotations, less 1 per cent trade discount on 100-barrel lots, with the right to deduct 1 per cent additional if invoice is made cash in 7 days; the advance to be without recourse to, or reclamation upon us, and to be due in any event.

2. The sugar when sold is to be billed in your name, although in fact as factor for us, and you shall without reclamation upon us,

at your own cost, pay all expenses, and assume all risks of the property, and of payment of collection. You are not to incur any expense on our account.

3. None of the sugar shall be sold or disposed of by you, either directly or indirectly, for less than our daily quotations with freight added from refining point to point of sale (as per equality rate book), nor on more liberal terms as to credit or cash discounts.

So long as the foregoing conditions are observed by you, we will, upon an affidavit to that effect, pay you a commission of three-sixteenth of a cent per pound, and in addition thereto you shall retain the profit, if any, over the advance made as above provided. In case of any failure to comply with either of the above conditions no commissions will be payable. Settlements will be made for each month's commissions at the expiration of 3 months thereafter. All commissions payable for the period preceding the 3 months will then become due. Payments will only be made as above.

This agency is terminable at the pleasure of either party on written notice.

Yours respectfully,

THE AMERICAN SUGAR REFINING COMPANY.

This rebate system still continues, but it appears not to be effectively enforced. Numerous jobbers have cut the prices of sugar, and those who maintain the agreement lose many customers. This change is not attributed to the competition of new refineries, but is charged by some witnesses to the failure of the jobbers themselves to keep faith, and by others to the carelessness of the American Sugar Refining Company in regard to enforcing the contract and requiring affidavits that goods have not been sold below the price fixed. Mr. Havemeyer says that the affidavit was abandoned by the trust, in 1897, on account of legislation against it, but adds that the agreement was never successfully enforced.

The general opinion appears to be

that the system is a legitimate and necessary one to prevent losses to dealers through excessive competition. Mr. SMITH specifically states that he believes the system is honorable, just, and legal. Without it dealers are compelled to perform a public service in distributing goods without a reasonable compensation, which is against public policy. Experience has proved this repeatedly.

The agreement as to rebates has never stipulated that jobbers shall not handle the products of other refineries. In fact, the various competing refineries have themselves copied the system. Thus Mr. THURBER states that the members of the Wholesale Grocers' Association are not confined to buying sugar from the American Sugar Refining Company. They buy as they choose, having now 5 different sources of supply, and have the same rebates from all companies.

Mr. JARVIE also knows of no contract by which wholesale grocers are restricted to handling the product of American Sugar Refining Company. Arbuckle Brothers sell through wholesale dealers exclusively, giving a rebate of three-sixteenths cent in addition to ordinary trade discounts. No affidavit is required.

A modification of the rebate system has recently been established in Ohio, owing to decisions of the courts against the rebate system. In May, 1899, the wholesale grocers adopted a plan among themselves designed to prevent cutting and to equalize prices according to freight rates. The plan is essentially to divide the State into six sections, and in case it is proved that prices have been cut to any retailer, all wholesale grocers in that section are required to reduce their price correspondingly to the place in question, taking away all profit and placing all on an equal footing. A circular stating the plan in full is quoted. A similar plan has been in operation in Illinois, and has helped to keep prices up to profitable rates.

Gustavus Myers: THEY PLUNDER THE TREASURY

In contrast with much of the testimony given before the Industrial Commission is the Muckraking attack on the Sugar Trust by Gustavus Myers (1872–1942). Myers began his writing career early, working for the Philadelphia Record *at the age of 18. He then graduated to New York City newspapers and emerged as a free-lance critical commentator on the American scene. One of his early books was a* History of Tammany Hall *(1901). Myers began research on his major work,* The History of the Great American Fortunes, *years before its final appearance (delayed by timid publishers) in 1910. In later life he resented the image of America abroad which in part his own critical works had helped to create. In 1935 his* America Strikes Back *came as a strong denial of the belief that American justice and national policies were more corrupt than those of Europe, or that the United States had any monopoly on "materialism." Myers' last major book was his* History of Bigotry in the United States, *published posthumously in 1943.*

The selection below comes from the concluding section of the revised (1936) edition of The History of the Great American Fortunes. *Myers condemns the Sugar Trust for corrupting politics and for criminally defrauding the United States Customs. More important for the stock-juggling and price-fixing charges commonly brought against business leaders, he accuses the Havemeyer combination of "profiteering."*

THE POLITICS OF BUSINESS

THE Sherman Anti-Trust law as well as other laws were indifferently brushed aside by the magnates rushing forward to organize trusts; only a year after the enactment of the Sherman Anti-Trust law, the Havemeyers and associates formed the American Sugar Refining Company, a combination of one hundred and twenty-one plants. From their sugar refinery, that of Havemeyer & Elder, the Havemeyers had already become multi-millionaires, and their fortune and the fortunes of their associates were enormously enhanced by the inordinate profits of the Sugar Trust. While the Rockefellers and their colleagues ever maintained a policy of profound silence, acknowledging nothing and disclosing nothing, Henry O. Havemeyer frankly, realistically admitted before a special committee of the United States Senate, in 1894, that trusts, railroad companies, corporations of all kinds, and rich individuals periodically contributed large amounts for campaign election purposes; such "politics of business," he testified, was the custom of "every individual and corporation or firm, trust or whatever you like to call it." Always in State campaigns, he further testified, the dominant party received the contribution.

The corruption was widespread and continuous. In return, official favors and immunity from molestation, or at any rate from serious prosecution was ex-pected — and was given. And in such cases as disclosures and the indignation of public opinion forced officials to take some action, the result did not inconvenience the money magnates. This fact was illustrated by many cases, one of which is here to the point. In a previous chapter we have passingly referred to the great custom-house frauds committed for the benefit of the combination called the Sugar Trust, but now that we are specifically touching upon the origin of the Havemeyer and other fortunes from that industry, an extensive elucidation is called for. Under the caption "Frauds upon the Revenue," the 1909 Annual Report of the Attorney-General of the United States (pp. 11 and 12) gave this account:

THE SUGAR INDUSTRY AND FRAUD

"An investigation was undertaken during the year 1907 into certain alleged frauds upon the Government in the underweighing of sugars imported into the United States by the American Sugar Refining Company and its predecessor, Messrs. Havemeyer & Elder. This investigation resulted, among other things, in a suit by the United States against the American Sugar Refining Company based upon proof of systematic frauds practiced in the weighing of sugars on the docks of the Havemeyer & Elder refineries in Brooklyn, N. Y., between the years 1901 and 1907."

As a matter of fact, it may be interpolated, the Custom House records published by the Sun of New York — then a morning newspaper — on November 11, 1909, showed that the frauds had been going on for at least two decades. The Sun's front-page, nine-column article, running over to the second page, giving the evidence, began: "The Sugar Trust has stolen boldly and enormously, as the subjoined article shows, from the United States Treasury for at least twenty years. It stole with the assistance of officials employed by the United States. It was nursed and protected in its stealings by powerful politicians. . . Those who knew that the Sugar Trust was a thief and who sought for legal proof in the Custom House records were referred to the thief itself. . . . The facts show that the Sugar Trust could not have stolen upwards of $30,000,000 without the cognizance of Treasury officials and the patronage of politicians. . . . It stole from 5 to 10 per cent of the duty on every cargo. . . . The Sugar Trust's power was such that it secured a special rate of estimating duties. This enabled it to juggle figures in the New York Custom House. . . . Shippers of sugar the world over knew of this robbery. Carriers knew it. Weighers knew it. Officials within the Custom House itself must have known it. The Sugar Trust silenced revelations." Further, the article declared, the $30,000,000 that the American Sugar Refining Company had stolen in 20 years had been done "with the assistance and connivance of powerful and petty politicians," including men of both of the old political parties who "shared in the plunder."

Returning to the U. S. Attorney-General's Report we find this record: "The evidence in the suit revealed a long-continued system of defrauding the Government, of unparalleled depravity."

The Government obtained a judgment. This resulted, late in April, 1909, "in the making of a compromise whereby the company paid to the Government the amount of the judgment of $134,411.03, and in addition the sum of $2,000,000, on account of duties fraudulently withheld by it on account of short-weighing of sugar imported by the American Sugar Refining Company of New York and the American Sugar Refining Company at the Havemeyer & Elder Refineries in Brooklyn or at its Jersey City refinery. This compromise was approved by the Secretary of the Treasury and by this department, and was accepted in full settlement of all *civil* liabilities. . . ."

GREAT THEFTS COMPROMISED

In its article the Sun ridiculed the trivial judgment thus accepted from a corporation capitalized at $90,000,000. It pointed out that the Federal District Attorney, in his opening address to the same jury which accorded the judgment, had declared that the Government could have asked for a far greater sum on Custom House entries in the previous three years, a period not covered by the statute of limitations. For it was upon this statute that the American Sugar Refining Company was able to base its main defense against full restitution. Even so, the Sun article stated, counsel for the company had informed its directors that a total of $9,000,000 could have been demanded.

But what of criminal proceedings? In making the settlement the Government had expressly reserved the right to prosecute all individuals responsible, "even" went on the U. S. Attorney-General's Report with a deferential tone, "if such individuals were officers of the company." His report continued: "The evidence has disclosed a network of corruption, not confined to the American Sugar Company, extending over a period of years, affecting both importers and officers of the Government, and it is as yet premature to state the precise extent of the conspiracy or the amount of the revenue of which the Government has been defrauded." Yet he feared "that the statute of limitations may have run in favor of many of the malefactors who are responsible for these frauds."

But who in this case were criminally prosecuted and were convicted? A few employees. Henry O. Havemeyer had died in 1907; besides dominating the sugar industry he had been a power in the world of finance as a director of the National City Bank. But other directors and officers of the American Sugar Refining Company could have been reached by law. Not one was incommoded by a criminal process, and the Sugar Trust kept on its flourishing way deriving continuous great profits from a high tariff and from secret low freight rates from railroads enabling it to overreach competitors. And, of course, there were the usual trust stock waterings and manipulations.

Public agitation kept demanding punishment of the "men higher up" in the Sugar Trust responsible for the frauds practiced upon the Government. The principals of the American Sugar Refining Company were, obviously enough, a matter of record, but in a singular expedition purporting to be an effort to find out the identity of the chief culprits,

a House of Representatives investigating committee, in 1911, incidentally brought out information as to stock juggling. The head of a nominally separate but subsidiary company of the American Sugar Refining Company testified that he himself had issued $10,000,000 of the common stock of that company to Henry O. Havemeyer without any cash consideration. Havemeyer lived in a spacious Fifth Avenue mansion and became renowned as an "art connoisseur and collector." There was considerable mystery about his will; his lawyers filed only a memorandum and not the will itself; evidently they wanted to withhold from the public the amount of the actual estate he left. The only information given was that the will contained no public bequests; that the entire estate was given in trust for the benefit of his three children; and that $50,000 yearly was given to his widow during her life. A valuation of his estate, made in 1910 by State Appraisers, showed that the value of ascertainable property in his possession at the time of his death was $14,500,000. His family presented his art collection to the Metropolitan Museum of Art. These are only a few illuminating facts regarding the sugar industry and its developing trust from which a number of multimillionaire fortunes have come. In World War and post-World War years when, as we have said, there was widespread great profiteering, the American Sugar Refining Company's dividends on its common stock ran from 8½ to 10 per cent.

IV. THE ROBBER BARONS AS PIONEERS

Edward Sherwood Meade: CARNEGIE INNOVATES

The economist Edward Sherwood Meade (in later life spelled Mead), (1874–   ), was an older colleague of the revisionist biographer of Jay Gould, Julius Grodinsky, at the University of Pennsylvania. There at the Wharton School, Meade taught finance for many years. Among his books were Trust Finance *(1903), a study of the origins and management of industrial combinations;* The Story of Gold *(1908); and* Corporation Finance *(1910), which became a standard textbook for years, going into a seventh edition in 1933 before being revised and retitled as a collaborative text in 1941* (The Business Corporation). *In 1939 Meade also wrote, with Grodinsky,* The Ebb and Flow of Investment Values. *Meade's corporation textbook was based originally on his many journal articles, of which the following extract was part of an early one (1901). In this reading he traces the growth of the Carnegie steel enterprise, and directly attributes its success to Carnegie's own foresight and genius.*

IN 1882 the Carnegie Steel Company (then Carnegie, Phipps & Co.) had inaugurated a policy whose object was to control all the factors which contributed to the production of steel, from the ore and coal in the ground to the steel billet and the steel rail. The purchase of a controlling interest in the stock of the H. C. Frick Coke Company, the largest owner of coal lands and the largest producer of coke in the Connellsville region, insured to Carnegie, Phipps & Co., besides a majority share in the earnings from the sale of coke in the open market, a supply of coke at prices so close to the cost of production as in later years to be a matter of legal complaint from the minority stockholders. In 1899 the Frick Coke Company owned fully two-thirds of the coal still remaining in the Connellsville region. The Carnegie Company also leased 98,000 acres of natural gas land in Western Pennsylvania, and purchased valuable limestone quarries in the Pittsburg district, securing by these several purchases an independent supply of fuel and fluxing material, and adding to the earnings of their steel mills the profits on the production of these materials. The Carnegie Company was also active in obtaining control of its ore supply and its transportation facilities. By the purchase in 1896 of a five-sixths interest in the stock of Oliver Iron Mining Company, which controlled large ore deposits in the Gogebic and Marquette ranges, — holdings which have since been greatly increased, — and by a fifty year contract made in 1897 with the Rockefeller iron mining and transportation companies, by which the Carnegie Company agreed to pay a royalty of $1.05 per ton for a yearly supply of 1,500,000 tons of soft ore de-

From E. S. Meade, "The Genesis of the United States Steel Corporation," *Quarterly Journal of Economics,* Vol. XV (August, 1901), pp. 532–541.

livered on shipboard, and a further maximum payment of 80 cents per ton for the transportation of this ore to the lower lake ports, the Carnegie Company secured an abundant supply of both hard and soft ores at prices which were not only more stable than those of the open market, but which were lower than the prices paid by outside companies. The Carnegie Company also purchased a controlling interest in the Pittsburg Steamship Company, which owned in 1900 11 steamships and 2 tugboats, with 6 additional steamers under construction. It also secured control of the Pittsburg, Bessemer & Lake Erie Railroad, extending from Conneaut, Ohio, where large docks were built and ore-handling machinery installed, to the Carnegie Mills at Duquesne. This railroad was reballasted with cinder from the blast furnaces, and relaid with 100-pound rails. The equipment was replaced by the first steel cars used in the United States, and by the heaviest engines. Through these several improvements the cost of transportation was reduced to 1 mill per ton mile, the lowest cost with one exception[1] of any railroad in the world. The ownership of an ore fleet made the Carnegie Company independent of the wide fluctuations in lake rates, and their control of the railroad gave them transportation at cost; for the Pittsburg, Bessemer & Lake Erie Railroad until last year had paid no dividends. By the close of 1897, the Carnegie Company was almost completely self-sufficient in all the factors of production. The profits which competitors added to their costs were added to its earnings; and the possession of these advantages, along with the admirable equipment of its furnaces and mills, gave

[1] The Duluth, Mesaba & Northern, controlled by the Rockefellers.

to the Carnegie Company the foremost position in the iron and steel trade of the United States, if not in the world.

The lessons of this example were not lost upon the leaders in the iron and steel consolidations of 1898 and 1899. No sooner were the new companies fairly upon their feet, and had realized the necessity of greater economy, than they began a movement which looked toward the attainment of an independence in raw materials similar to that which the Carnegie Company had already achieved. . . .

These projects of industrial independence were rapidly taking form during 1900, and their approaching consummation menaced the continuance of harmony in the steel trade. In the West, the Federal Steel Company was faced with the danger of losing its entire market for wire rods, and in the Ohio district with the loss of a large demand for the output of its Lorain plant. In the Pittsburg district, the Carnegie Company was affected by each one of the developments in that section. The American Steel and Wire, the Moore Companies, and the National Tube Company were each striving to make themselves independent of the Carnegie Company, which had, from the beginning, found its largest market in the mills which its would-be rivals now controlled. If their plans should materialize, the Carnegie Company would have to find new markets for its blooms and billets, — markets much more difficult to approach than the Pittsburg district afforded. Its former customers would produce for themselves the enormous quantity of material which they had formerly purchased. The tendency of the iron and steel industry, under the leadership of the consolidations, was towards a declaration of industrial independence, which would leave the Carnegie and the Federal Steel Companies to blaze new avenues of demand.

Neither of these companies, however, had any intention of submitting to such a loss of markets. They had long since determined — in the case of the Carnegie Company, according to Mr. Schwab, in the early part of 1900 — to resist the new policy by direct competition. If the other large companies refused to buy their steel billets, they would convert those steel billets into wire rods, sheets, and tubes, and sell them in competition with their recalcitrant customers, — in other words, they would seek their new markets, not in foreign lands or in new forms of production, but in the preserves of their rivals.

The Federal Steel Company led off in this counter-movement by threatening to build wire mills unless the American Steel and Wire Company should abandon its plan of producing its own material and renew its wire-rod contract with the Federal Steel Company. The Steel and Wire Company saw no present profit in competition, and its Western extensions were abandoned. With the situation in the Pittsburg district, the Carnegie Company proposed to deal in similar fashion. On January 12, 1901, this company announced the proposed construction of a large tube mill at Conneaut, Ohio, having chosen this location on Lake Erie both because of the railway discrimination against Pittsburg in east-bound freights, and because the empty ore cars returning from Pittsburg could be filled with coke for the tube works. They also proposed to build sheet mills at Homestead; and it was strongly intimated that other lines of finished material would be invaded. At the same time, the Carnegie Company was preparing to secure an independent line to the seaboard by way of the Western Maryland Railroad, and the abandoned route of the South Pennsylvania. These announcements caused the most serious anxiety to the leaders of the newly formed consolidations in the Central West. In the Chicago district, it was generally believed that the carrying out of the plans of independence conceived by the management of the American Steel and Wire Company had only been postponed to a more favorable season. The fighting strength of the two companies involved was so nearly equal that permanent peace could not be expected in view of the large inducements offered by independent control of the materials of production. At any time the harmony in the steel trade of this section might be destroyed, and monopoly earnings reduced to a competitive basis. In the Pittsburg district, the Carnegie Company threatened with its competition the five Moore Companies, the Steel and Wire Company, and the National Tube Company. There was a general belief in the sincerity of Mr. Carnegie's emphatic declarations, and the future of harmonious control in the Pittsburg district appeared very doubtful. The iron and steel trade of the Middle West seemed about to descend into the depths of a competitive struggle, wherein the seller, who for a short time had been the master of the buyer, should again be his servant. Such a contingency it was to the paramount interest of the consolidations to avoid.

The situation in the Pittsburg district was of peculiar menace. The Carnegie Steel Company owned the most complete, the best-equipped, and the best-managed steel plant in the United States. The perfection of its equipment in point of independent supplies of materials and transportation service has been already described. No one of its rivals was worthy to be compared with it in point of self-sufficiency of production. This equipment supplied ore and fuel to the mills which were grouped so closely about Pittsburg that the president of the company was able to visit some department of each mill on successive days. The Edgar Thompson furnaces and mills were at Bessemer, two miles from Pittsburg; the Duquesne furnaces and mills, four miles from Pittsburg; and the Homestead Steel Works, one mile from the city. Besides these larger works, there was located in or immediately adjoining the city the upper and lower Union Mills, the Carrie and Lucy Furnaces, and the Howard Axle Works. All these plants were connected by the Union Railway, with thirty-nine miles of track, which in turn connected with the Pittsburg, Bessemer & Lake Erie Railroad to the north. This arrangement of mines, coke ovens, and mills, was the most favorable that could have been devised for economical production. The mills of the Carnegie Steel Company were concentrated at the point of largest present advantage, where materials could be most easily assembled, and from which the largest markets could be most easily reached. It was this fact of concentration, even more than their superior facilities, which gave to the Carnegie Company their most pronounced advantage. The mills of their rivals were too widely scattered. Their location antedated the recognition of Pittsburg as the natural seat of the iron and steel trade. For example, the plants of the National Steel Company were at Youngstown, Columbus, Bellaire Mills and Mingo Junction in Ohio, and at New Castle, Sharon, and Uniontown in Pennsylvania. Only in one instance — Youngstown and Niles being but fifteen miles apart — were two plants within hailing

distance, and some of them were two hundred miles apart. All of these plants could not have equal advantages in obtaining materials, and no one of them was so well situated as the mills at Pittsburg. The plants of the National Tube Company were even more scattered, and those of the American Steel and Wire were sown broadcast over the whole face of the land. A grant of land, a cash bonus, ten years' exemption from taxation, a local connection, any one of a number of causes entirely disconnected from considerations of economic production, had determined the original location of these plants, the burden of whose maladjustment the steel trusts had now to assume and carry. The plan of concentration on Neville's Island, which the American Steel and Wire Company had already begun to execute, was an evident recognition, on their part, of the superior economy of concentrated production in power, in labor, in superintendence, and in the provision of materials. Mr. Carnegie had anticipated his rivals by twenty years. All the benefits of centralization which they were striving for he had long since achieved.

The advantages of the Carnegie Company did not stop here. Their mechanical equipment was superior to that of any other mills, and their business was the best managed of any in the country. . . .

The superior equipment of the Carnegie works was the result of a policy of large expenditure upon betterments persistently pursued for many years. "Every new process and every new machine which would in any way increase the efficiency, reduce the cost, and improve the product of the Carnegie Company, has been applied, until this great concern has raised the physical condition of its plants to a point which is unsurpassed." Dividends had never been considered by the management. Improvement had been the one thing thought of. During the years 1898 and 1899 the Carnegie Company expended out of earnings, upon new construction and betterments, no less a sum than $20,000,000. The nature of this policy of the investment of earnings in improvements may be illustrated by comparative statement of the Homestead mills in 1890 and 1898:

1890

1. Two 5-ton Bessemer converters.
2. Seven open-hearth furnaces, one 15-ton, four 20-ton, two 35-ton.
3. One 28-inch blooming mill.
4. One 23-inch and one 33-inch train for structural shapes.
5. One 10-inch mill.
6. One 32-inch slabbing mill for rolling heavy ingots.
7. One 120-inch plate mill.
   Annual capacity, 295,000 tons.

1898

1. Three Bessemer converters, two 10-ton, one 12-ton.
2. Thirty open-hearth furnaces, one 12-ton, six 25-ton, eight 35-ton, and fifteen 40-ton.
3. One 28-inch and one 38-inch blooming mill.
4. One 23-inch and one 33-inch train for structural shapes.
5. One 10-inch mill.
6. One 32-inch slabbing machine.
7. One 40-inch cogging mill.
8. One 35-inch beam mill.
9. One 119-inch plate mill.
10. One 3,000-ton and one 10,000-ton hydraulic press.
11. Steel foundry, press shop, and machine shop.
    Annual capacity, 2,260,000 tons.

These represent the improvements at only one of the Carnegie plants, made during a season of depression and paid for out of earnings. The increased earning power here represented was clear gain. No deductions had to be made for interest payments. The policy of the Carnegie Company was purely industrial. Financial considerations had little weight. Its shares were never in the market. It had no loans to float, no stock commissions to sell, no bonuses to dispose of. The greater part of its profits was each year invested in the plant. As Mr. Carnegie recently remarked, he and his partners knew little about the manufacture of stocks and bonds. They were only conversant with the manufacture of steel.

The management of the Carnegie Company represented the acme of productive efficiency.

/J. H. Bridge: CARNEGIE HESITATES

In the controversial selection which follows we see a very different vision of Andrew Carnegie, published only two years after Meade's tribute. The author, J. H. Bridge (1856–1939) was, like Carnegie, a British immigrant and a prolific writer. Bridge produced nine or ten

From J. H. Bridge, *Inside History of the Carnegie Steel Company* (New York, 1903), pp. 32–48.

books and was Curator of the Frick Art Gallery from 1914 until his death. His interest in Carnegie was not impartial or scholarly. Bridge had been secretary to Carnegie's English friend, the laissez-faire *philosopher Herbert Spencer, before Carnegie brought him over to the United States to work as his own "literary assistant." In 1889 Bridge broke away from his employer, and in 1903 his* Inside History of the Carnegie Steel Company *lashed out at Carnegie, belittling him both as a businessman and as an innovator. The lazy, overcautious, and hesitant Carnegie of this account seems the negation of the entrepreneurial virtues.*

[*Carnegie is slow to take up a new slabbing-mill, invented by a German immigrant called Zimmer*]

THE mill described by Zimmer consisted of a pair of horizontal rolls similar to the ordinary plate-mill then in use, but having in addition two movable vertical rolls that could be opened or closed at the will of the operator. Mr. Kloman was at once struck with the value of the improvement, especially for rolling material for bridge orders; and with Zimmer's aid he erected the first German mill in the country. This is the machine now known in the trade as the Universal Mill. It was capable of rolling plates from seven to twenty-four inches wide, and from three-sixteenths to two inches in thickness, with rolled edges. From the first day this mill was a mechanical success, and was the forerunner of several improved mills of the same character afterwards erected at the Upper Mill and at Homestead. Indeed, the great slabbing-mill which was erected at Homestead in 1888 was a lineal descendant of the little Zimmer mill built in 1867–68 at Kloman's. This slabbing-mill now turns out thirty thousand tons of steel slabs a month; and, as it has steadily increased its production from year to year, it seems probable that its limit has not been reached even yet. Before its erection the average weight of an ingot

that could be used to make plates direct was about one ton; whereas ten- and fifteen-ton ingots are now rolled down to a thickness of four to six inches, then cut while red-hot into the lengths needed at the plate-mill.

This little idea of the German workman has been worth millions of dollars to the firm that imported him to take the place of a striker. As for Zimmer himself, his reward was a well-paid position as foreman of the mill he erected and of its improved successors. He accumulated a competence, and was believed to be possessed of upwards of one hundred thousand dollars before he died.

Despite the vaunted progressiveness of the American manufacturer, these machines, open to the inspection of anybody who passed through the Union Mills, were but slowly adopted by other firms. Even Andrew Carnegie, after twenty years' experience of the excellencies of the German mill, in consonance with his dictum, "Pioneering don't pay," opposed the erection of the slabbing-mill at Homestead; although he afterwards became an enthusiastic admirer of its work. . . .

[*Carnegie is also slow to adopt the Bessemer process, and his claim of pioneering in the building of iron bridges is refuted*]

. . . Piper and Shiffler had been extensively engaged in building bridges of wood and iron for at least eight years prior to the formation of the Keystone Bridge Company. Andrew Carnegie, however, in his account of the business, speaks as though it originated with the Keystone Bridge Company, which he represents as his personal creation. In a short biography which he recently published through the S. S. McClure Newspaper Syndicate, he says:

There were so many delays on railroads in those days from burned or broken wooden bridges that I felt the day of wooden bridges must end soon, just as the day of wood-burning locomotives was ended. Cast iron bridges, I thought, ought to replace them, so I organized a company, principally from railroad men I knew to make these iron bridges, and we called it the Keystone Bridge Company. Development of this company required my time, so I resigned from the railroad service in 1867.

Mr. Carnegie has an excellent verbal memory; but he is especially prone to error when recalling events. He is, in fact, constantly mistaking impressions for occurrences, as in this case. That it is his memory which is here at fault is shown by a further error in the same biography. Speaking of his entry upon the manufacture of Bessemer steel he says:

On my return from England [he is speaking of the year 1868] I built at Pittsburg a plant for the Bessemer process of steel-making, which had not until then been operated in this country, and started in to make steel rails for American railroads.

First noting that the construction of the first Carnegie Bessemer steel plant was not commenced until April, 1873, and was not in operation until the end of August, 1875, it may be seen by reference to any cyclopedia that the first

Bessemer steel produced in America was made at Wyandotte, Michigan, in 1864, and that the first Bessemer steel rails made in America were rolled at the North Chicago Rolling Mill in presence of the American Iron and Steel Institute in May, 1865, from ingots made at Wyandotte. Some of these rails were laid in the track of one of the railroads running out of Chicago; and were still in use ten years afterwards when the Carnegie firm made its first Bessemer steel. Even if Mr. Carnegie's recollection had been correct as to the date of this visit to England, it would still be at fault in respect to the beginnings of Bessemer steel rails in America; for there were produced no less than 7,225 tons of such rails in America in 1868. The prosaic fact is that the earliest of the Carnegie steel enterprises was the eleventh in America instead of the first to use the Bessemer process.

In themselves these discrepancies are of little moment. It is probable that not one reader in a hundred would notice them; but the author deems it his duty to the exceptional reader to set forth the facts as he finds them.

The Keystone Bridge Company, then, was simply the incorporated business of Messrs. Piper and Shiffler. Carnegie, through his official position on the railroad, had long been familiar with their work; and he had known Piper since 1858, when the latter was employed for a time in the car shops at Altoona, where Carnegie then lived.

Piper was a mechanical genius who was always inventing things. One of his patents, still remembered by his associates of that day, was a turn-table for locomotives; and he afterwards embodied some of the ideas it contained in a drawbridge. He also devised an improved bridge-post which was extensively used; and there were other things invented in conjunction with Linville, who was bridge engineer for the Pennsylvania Railroad, and later became president of the Keystone Bridge Company. . . .

Shiffler, the other founder of the business, had worked with Piper in a contractor's gang under the firm of Stone, Quigley & Co. on the Pennsylvania lines prior to 1857. This was the period referred to by Chief Engineer Wilson, when he said he had known them "for some years" prior to 1857 while "erecting bridges for the Pennsylvania Rail Road." Here they got the experience which made their firm so successful, and qualified them for the direction of the Keystone Bridge Company when that was formed. But neither of them originated the use of iron in bridges; for this material had been so used from the earliest days. . . .

Thus, so far from being the pioneer in the iron railroad bridge business, Mr.

Carnegie occupied a position a long way down the list. When he finally did become interested with Piper and Shiffler it was not, as he alleges, in "cast-iron bridges." When cast iron was in vogue for bridge structures in England, wood was used in America; and when wood was replaced with iron it was wrought iron, and later Bessemer steel, that was used. The only parts of Piper & Shiffler's bridges that were of cast iron were Piper's patent posts; and these were a very small part of the whole, which, of course, was of wrought iron.

It is also worthy of mention that Andrew Carnegie's principal interest in the Keystone Bridge Company was given to him in return for services rendered in its promotion. He paid no cash for any of his shares; but desiring to have a larger holding than that gratuitously assigned to him, he gave his note to the company in payment of the increased interest, and the first four dividends sufficed to liquidate the debt.

Charles Edward Russell: THE BEEF TRUST GROWS FAT

Meatpacking was America's leading industry (in value of total product) by 1914. The industry was dominated by great names — the "Beef Barons," Swift, Armour, Morris — and had been bitterly attacked by journalists as well as by Upton Sinclair's grim novel of the Chicago stockyards, The Jungle *(1906). Charles Edward Russell (1860–1941), a well-known journalist in the 90's, and sometime Socialist Party candidate (expelled for supporting the United States' entry into World War I), in this extract from his* The Greatest Trust in the World *(1905) gives a sweeping indictment of the meatpacking leaders and a dramatic picture of the far-reaching nature of their economic and social influence.*

IN the free republic of the United States of America is a power greater than the government, greater than the courts or judges, greater than legislatures, superior to and independent of all authority of state or nation.

From Charles Edward Russell, *The Greatest Trust in the World* (New York, 1905), pp. 1–6.

It is a greater power than in the history of men has been exercised by king, emperor, or irresponsible oligarchy. In a democracy it has established a practical empire more important than Tamerlaine's and ruled with a sway as certain. In a country of law, it exists and proceeds in defiance of law. In a country historically proud of its institutions it establishes unchecked a condition that refutes and nullifies the significance of those institutions. We have grown familiar in this country with many phases of the mania of money-getting, and the evil it may work to mankind at large; we have seen none so strange and alarming as this of which I write. Names change, details change; but when the facts of these actual conditions are laid bare it will puzzle a thoughtful man to say wherein the rule of the great power now to be described differs in any essential from the rule of a feudal tyrant in the darkness of the Middle Ages.

Three times a day this power comes to the table of every household in America, rich or poor, great or small, known or unknown; it comes there and extorts its tribute. It crosses the ocean and makes its presence felt in multitudes of homes that would not know how to give it a name. It controls prices and regulates traffic in a thousand markets. It changes conditions and builds up and pulls down industries; it makes men poor or rich as it will; it controls or establishes or obliterates vast enterprises across the civilized circuit. Its lightest word affects men on the plains of Argentina or the by-streets of London.

Of some of the most important industries of this country it has an absolute, iron-clad, infrangible monopoly; of others it has a control that for practical purposes of profit is not less complete. It fixes at its own will the price of every pound of fresh, salted, smoked, or preserved meat prepared and sold in the United States. It fixes the price of every ham, every pound of bacon, every pound of lard, every can of prepared soup. It has an absolute monopoly of our enormous meat exports, dressed and preserved. It has an absolute monopoly of the American trade in fertilizers, hides, bristles, horn and bone products. It owns or controls or dominates every slaughter-house except a few that have inconsiderable local or special trades. It owns steam and electric railroads, it owns the entire trolley-car service in several cities, and is acquiring the like property elsewhere. It owns factories, shops, stock-yards, mills, land and land companies, plants, warehouses, politicians, legislators, and Congressmen.

It defies Wall Street and all that therein is. It terrorizes great railroad corporations long used to terrorizing others. It takes toll from big and little, it gouges millions from railroad companies, and cent pieces from obscure shippers. To-day it is compelling a lordly railroad to dismiss its general manager, to-morrow it is black-listing and ruining some little commission merchant. It is remorseless, tireless, greedy, insatiable, and it plans achievements so much greater than any so far recorded in the history of commerce that the imagination flags in trying to follow its future possibilities.

It fixes, for its own profit, the prices the farmer of the West shall receive for his cattle and hogs, and the prices the butcher of the East shall charge for his meat.

It fixes the prices that the grower of California shall receive for his fruit, and the price the laborer of New York shall pay for his breakfast.

It lays hands upon the melon-grower

of Colorado and the cotton-grower of Georgia, and compels each to share with it the scanty proceeds of his toil.

It can affect the cost of living in Aberdeen and Geneva as easily as in Chicago and New York.

It has in the last three years increased, for its own benefit, the expenses of every household in America. It controls or influences the prices of one-half the food consumed by the nation. It has its share in the proceeds of more commodities of daily consumption than all other trusts, combinations, and monopolies together, and the prices of these it seeks to augment for its own profit.

It can make, within certain limits, the price of wheat, of corn, of oats, what it pleases; it will shortly be able to control the price of every loaf of bread.

Its operations have impoverished or ruined farmers and stockmen, destroyed millions of investments, caused banks to break and men to commit suicide, precipitated strikes, and annihilated industries.

So great is the terror it inspires in some quarters that citizens under the constitutional guaranties of freedom do not dare, even in the privacy of their offices or homes, to speak a word that this power would not approve of, and multi-millionaires, railroad magnates, and captains of industry quail before it.

At every step of its progress it has violated national or state law, or both, and with impunity. It has been declared by federal and state courts to be an outlaw and to have no right to exist. It has gone steadily on strengthening its hold extending its lines, and multiplying its victims.

We are accustomed to think that the Standard Oil Company is the ultimate of monopolistic achievement; here is something compared with which the Standard Oil Company is puerile; here is something that affects a thousand lives where the Standard Oil Company affects one; here is something that promises greater fortunes and greater power than ten Standard Oil Companies. Reaching out, absorbing industry after industry, augmenting and building, by great brute strength and by insidious, intricate, hardly discoverable windings and turnings, day and night this monstrous thing grows and strengthens until its grip is at the nation's throat.

I am quite well aware that my words may seem extravagant to the generality of readers; to those who know the history and actual operations of the American Beef Trust they will appear an understatement of galling and humiliating truths.

And the most singular fact, the fact that should make all of us stop and think, is that the men that are exercising this incalculable power upon the lives and destinies of their fellow-creatures, are not bad men; as the world goes, they are very good men. They operate one of the most cruel and oppressive monopolies; they would not knowingly be cruel or unjust in any affair of personal conduct. The business they conduct is merely piracy on a gigantic scale; they are themselves kindly, generous, and upright. Like other men they have been driven along by an economic evolution beyond their knowledge or control. They are as certainly the victims of conditions as are the people on whose family tables the American Beef Trust grows fat.

Charles Kuhlmann: THE BEEF BARONS REVOLUTIONIZE THE FOOD INDUSTRY

Charles B. Kuhlmann retired from the Economics Department of Hamline University, St. Paul, Minnesota in 1952 after many years of teaching and study. He had won the Hart, Schaffner, and Marx Prize for a book on the history of American flourmilling in 1929. In the following selection Professor Kuhlmann gives a succinct outline of the rise of the meatpacking industry. He emphasizes the introduction of major innovations by men like Swift and Armour as chief determinants of the industry's progress. A more total contrast to the Russell reading — in content, tone, and aim — could scarcely be possible.

U P to 1850, Chicago was not an important center of the meat packing industry. The territory north and west of the city was as yet but sparsely settled. There were no railroads into that area and only the lake steamers to give access to Eastern markets. In 1848 there were only six packing houses in Chicago, and their combined output was less than one-tenth that of the Cincinnati packers.

In 1848 the Illinois and Michigan Canal was completed, and in the same year the Chicago and Galena Railroad was opened to service. Together they brought prosperity to Chicago. Hog-raisers who formerly had driven their animals to local markets in central and northern Illinois now shipped them to the new center. The immediate financial success of the Chicago and Galena line inspired the building of other railroads to the Eastern markets and westward into new territory being opened up beyond the Mississippi. Improved transportation not only drew larger supplies of cattle and hogs to the Chicago market, but it stimulated shipments of meat to distant Eastern markets. Between 1852 and 1860 the number of cattle packed in Chicago doubled and the number of hogs slaughtered tripled. By 1864 Chicago had become the leading packing center of the country.

Of course, this growth was not due solely to the influence of transportation. In the decade after the Civil War many of the farmers in the Chicago territory changed from wheat raising to corn growing. The change-over was accelerated by the chinch-bug, by wheat-rust, and perhaps by "wheat-sick" land. Many farmers in the western part of the new Corn Belt found it profitable to buy range cattle and fatten them for the market. Pigs are a good side line for the cattle raisers: they can be combined with cattle because they eat what cattle waste and they can be pastured with the cattle. Consequently, the popularity of corn growing caused a phenomenal growth in the number of hogs raised in the Corn Belt states, especially after 1860.

By that date the railroads had opened up large areas west of the Mississippi for cattle raising. Cattle ranching has always been associated with frontier life. Great herds raised in Texas moved over

Harold F. Williamson, *Growth of the American Economy*, 2nd ed. © 1951. Reprinted by permission of Prentice-Hall, Inc.

the cattle trail to the northern ranges and then were shipped to Chicago for sale to the packers.

//A minor but not unimportant cause of the growth of packing in Chicago was the development of the Union Stock Yards. The slaughterhouses at first provided their own storage facilities: pens for the hogs, and pastures at the outskirts of the town for the cattle. Then the railroads established stockyards in various sections of the city, each railroad for a time having its own yard. In 1865 nine railroads combined to establish the Union Stock Yards. Covering 300 acres and containing facilities for unloading 500 cars at a time, they were the largest stockyards in the world. Both as a market for buying and selling livestock and as a system of physical distribution, they became a model for other yards that were established later in the newer centers.

In Chicago, as in Cincinnati, the packing industry was at first almost exclusively interested in hogs. Before the development of refrigeration, fresh beef could not be shipped any considerable distance except during the winter months. The demand for packed beef seldom exceeded 10 per cent of the beef supply. But anywhere from one-half to two-thirds of the hogs could be packed. Thus there was a larger steadier market for pork, and this was the more attractive branch of the industry, until refrigeration changed the picture.

New developments in packing are associated with the rise of the captains of industry in this field. Some of them were immigrants who had acquired experience in packing in Ireland, Germany, and other countries. Some were men who had started as cattle traders or packers in Eastern cities and then migrated to the West. Still others got their start in the Middle West. Perhaps the ablest of them all was Gustavus F. Swift, who had started as a New England cattle dealer and butcher. Located originally in Boston, he moved west as a cattle buyer first to Albany, then to Buffalo, and finally to Chicago. He started cattle buying in Chicago in 1875 and in 1877 established a packing plant.

Philip Armour started a produce and commission business in Milwaukee in 1859. Some three years later, with his brothers as partners, he started a grain business in Chicago, and at the same time became a partner of John Plankinton in a packing plant in Milwaukee. During the Civil War, Armour progressed rapidly, partly from the profits of a rising pork market and partly through speculative dealings in grain. In 1867 the firm of Armour & Company started packing hogs in Chicago. The partnership with Plankinton continued for a number of years longer, and then the firm was consolidated with Armour & Company.

A third notable packer was Nelson Morris, who came to Chicago in 1859. When the Chicago stockyards were established, he became an important cattle dealer. In the 1870's he made large shipments of live cattle to the European market and presently established a packing house. His was one of the first packing houses to be built near the Union Stock Yards. Gradually almost all the plants were moved into that neighborhood.

Whereas Armour and Morris were primarily interested in pork-packing, Swift concerned himself with the marketing of beef in the Eastern consuming centers. Boston, New York, and Philadelphia had local firms engaged in slaughtering and distributing fresh beef. These naturally tried to get shipments of live cattle from the West, but transportation was slow and facilities for handling livestock bad. A large proportion of the animals died on the way, and the shrinkage in the rest caused serious loss. Nor did the Eastern slaughterers operate on a scale sufficiently large to enable full utilization of by-products. Only about half of the animal could be used for meat; the rest (except the hide) was wasted. Swift saw that the remedy for these conditions was to be found in doing the slaughtering at Western centers and shipping fresh beef to the Eastern markets. For a time he confined his efforts to shipments during the winter months. It was the development of refrigeration that brought a revolution in the industry.

Refrigeration began in the slaughterhouses. Up to about 1860 even the slaughtering of hogs was confined to the winter months. Then the packers found it possible to slaughter successfully in warm weather by placing crates of ice and salt about the slaughterhouses. Wherever ice was cheap, it was possible to build large refrigerator chambers, so by 1870 all the larger plants had cooling rooms chilled with natural ice. Thus slaughtering could be carried on continuously through the year.

By that time Swift and other packers were experimenting with shipments in freight cars iced in various ways. Repeated failures did not daunt the persistent "Yankee of the Yards." Finally one of Swift's engineers discovered the principle of air circulation, as applied to refrigeration, and designed a practical refrigerator car. As soon as Swift had demonstrated its practicability, the other Chicago packers adopted it. By 1880 this type of car was being regularly used for shipments from the West. As a result, sales of fresh beef to Eastern markets rose with great rapidity. In

1875 Chicago packers had slaughtered 250,000 cattle. The number was doubled in 1880 and doubled again by 1890.

The packers had need to be persistent, for the new development met with a great deal of opposition. The Trunkline railroads refused to build refrigerator cars. They did not want to take the risk and undergo the expense while the cars were still an experiment. If the experiment proved successful, they would lose a large volume of traffic in cattle cars and in stockyards in Eastern markets. So Swift found it necessary to build his own refrigerator cars, and for some years he ran them to the Atlantic Seaboard over the Grand Trunk Railway of Canada, which was not a member of the Trunkline Association. Opposition came also from the local butchers. Many of them refused to handle Chicago beef. They tried to convince their customers that the refrigerated beef was inferior in quality if not altogether unfit for consumption. In some states the legislatures were induced to pass hostile legislation. Virginia, for example, required that all fresh meat offered for sale in that state must be slaughtered within one hundred miles of the place of consumption.

Shrewd management was able to overcome this opposition. Swift met the antagonism of the local butchers by setting up distributing firms in Eastern centers, in which he took local men into partnership. Armour and Morris set up branch houses from which to distribute their products. "The Swift partnerships were the best for immediate results but the branch house proved superior in the long run so that eventually Swift also adopted that method." Careful and persistent advertising slowly overcame the prejudice against Western beef, although for years it had to be sold in Eastern markets at lower prices than native beef.

The opposition of the railroads was overcome by the payment of proportionately higher freight rates on beef than on live cattle and by the willingness of the packers to assume the burden of providing and servicing the refrigerator cars.

The introduction of the refrigerator car accelerated the revolution in the packing industry. The packers could now set up an all-year industry and sell to a national market. To meet the demands of that market, they had to develop slaughtering and packing capacity to meet sudden or unusual demands. This meant large cold-storage facilities in which supplies could be accumulated for peak periods or withheld from the market when demand unexpectedly fell off. All these things involved heavy outlays, large capital, and an increase in the size of the business unit. Armour & Company, for example, showed a net worth of $200,000 in 1870. By 1880 this had risen to $2,500,000, and by 1890 the figure was $10,500,000. Large-scale production, in turn, created serious marketing problems for the packers. The refrigerator car put them into the transportation business. In order to avoid the waste of hauling empty cars back to their plants and in order to provide a full load for outbound shipments, it was necessary for the packers to engage in the buying and selling of various other products. Fruit, butter, eggs, cheese, and many sorts of vegetables were brought from every part of the country in the returning refrigerator cars. A marketing and storing organization had to be built up to handle these products, and thus the packers became produce merchants on a very large scale. Meantime the system of branch houses had been expanded, so that Armour, for example, had 40 such branches by 1890. To reach retailers distant from their branches, "peddler cars" were put in service and later automobile trucks were used.

The introduction of refrigeration also meant an expansion in the utilization of by-products. The local butcher threw away almost half of the animal because he had no plants to utilize such waste products. His scale of production was too small to justify an effort to use them. But the large-scale packer saw an opportunity in this waste. Even before 1875 there were plants in Chicago processing lard, lard oil, tallow, soap, glue, and fertilizer. These were allied industries rather than an integral part of the packing industry. After 1875 the packers took the manufacture of by-products into their own hands. Armour took over an established glue factory in 1884; somewhat later he began to make soap. A new invention made it possible to use fats, hitherto useless, for the making of oleomargarine. This became a thriving part of the industry by 1880. Then the packers set up research laboratories to study the problems of waste utilization. As a result one line of research has developed some 50 pharmaceutical and medical preparations. To find a market for some by-products, it was necessary to combine them with products of other industries, a development that led to further expansion. For example, to utilize the large quantities of glue they were producing, the packers engaged in the manufacture of sandpaper. In utilizing wastes, other wastes were created which, in turn, became raw materials for other by-products. Including merchandised as well as processed products, a modern packing house may sell nearly 700 different items.

Harold C. Passer: THE INVENTOR-BUSINESSMEN: WESTINGHOUSE AND EDISON

Harold C. Passer (1921–   ) is a practicing economist (Eastman Kodak) and consultant, trained at Harvard. In a learned book on the electrical industries, Dr. Passer traces the rise of Edison and Westinghouse, inventive geniuses who were also business leaders. They produced new goods mainly where the market demanded, and both of them founded large companies. Yet the problems they faced and the solutions they offered are a far cry from the interests and activities of Jay Gould or H. O. Havemeyer.

GEORGE WESTINGHOUSE received no formal education after the age of fourteen except during the three months he attended Union College, Schenectady, New York. His father operated a machine shop in Schenectady, where George worked for a number of years before and after his Civil War service. At the age of 21, in 1867, he invented a device for returning derailed railroad cars to the track and an improved form of railroad frog. With two partners, who each contributed $5,000, he organized a firm to market these inventions. He contracted with steel mills at Troy, New York, and Pompton, New Jersey, to manufacture them, while he acted as the company's salesman and called on railroads throughout the East and Middle West. In 1868, Westinghouse dissolved his Schenectady firm and shifted operations to Pittsburgh. The principal reason for this move was that in Pittsburgh he was able to have his car replacer manufactured more cheaply than before. Westinghouse's contact with the railroads had brought to his attention the need for an automatic power brake for railroad trains. He began work on this problem sometime in 1868, and in the early part of 1869, he invented the air brake. With the financial help of Ralph Baggley, a Pittsburgh foundry manager, Westinghouse constructed a complete air-brake unit and equipped a train for a trial run, which was held in April 1869. The test was a success. In September, the Westinghouse Air Brake Company was organized. Westinghouse became president; Baggley and five others, nearly all railroad men, made up the board of directors. The capitalization of the company was $500,000. Manufacturing operations were started in the factory which Baggley's foundry firm had occupied.

Westinghouse spent much time in England during the decade 1870–1880, selling his air brake to the English railroads and establishing manufacturing plants for the European market. He became interested in English signaling and switching devices, which were considerably in advance of those in use on American railroads, and finally decided to enter the switch and signal business. In 1881, he bought control of two companies, one a Pennsylvania company and the other a Massachusetts company, which he combined to form the Union

Switch and Signal Company. The company headquarters and manufacturing plant were established at Pittsburgh. Within a few years, Westinghouse invented a number of automatic switching and signaling devices for his new firm. In these inventions, he combined a force familiar to him, compressed air, with a force new to him, electricity.

The experiences of Westinghouse up to 1881 were good preparation for his entrance into electrical manufacturing. His work in the air brake gave him inventive, manufacturing, and marketing experience. Beyond that, the air brake became the basis of future financial support, both directly from profits and indirectly from the reputation Westinghouse had achieved. The Union Switch and Signal Company, with its engineering staff, manufacturing facilities, and electrical devices, was to be the organization which Westinghouse could use to begin electrical manufacturing.

One other of his many activities played an important part in his preparation for electrical manufacturing. That activity was his work in natural gas. It was well known that natural gas was plentiful in the Pittsburgh area, but because the gas was under enormous pressure and had no odor, it was difficult and dangerous to handle. Almost no attempt had been made to commercialize it. Westinghouse studied the gas problem and thought he could devise ways to handle it safely and economically. In 1883, he drilled a well on the grounds of his Pittsburgh estate and discovered a large amount of gas under very high pressure. After he had the gas under control, he formed the Philadelphia Company, which distributed gas to factories and residences in the Pittsburgh area for many years.

Westinghouse made many technical contributions to the art of handling gas. Among the most important was his system of conveying gas over relatively long distances. The high pressure at the well could force large quantities of gas through small and inexpensive pipes for distances up to four and five miles. But such a high pressure could not be utilized by the gas consumer. To reduce the pressure to the level which was safe for ordinary use, Westinghouse widened the pipes near the place of gas consumption. The concept of a gas-distribution system which uses high pressure for transmission and has a device to convert this high pressure into usable low pressure for consumption is analogous to the concept of an electrical distribution system which uses high voltage for transmission and has a device to convert this high voltage into usable low voltage for consumption. The pressure-reducing device in the gas system was the large-diameter pipe. The pressure-reducing device in the electrical system was to be the transformer. The success of Westinghouse in developing a high-pressure system of gas distribution gave him confidence in his ability to achieve similar success in developing the alternating-current system of electrical distribution.

When Westinghouse first contemplated entering the electrical industry, he decided to investigate incandescent lighting. He assigned several of the electrical engineers of the Union Switch and Signal Company to the problem and carried on studies of his own. His brother, H. H. Westinghouse, was at that time manufacturing a high-speed steam engine he had invented. The engine was suitable for driving dynamos, and in the course of his business activities, H. H. Westinghouse came into contact with an electrical engineer, William Stanley. Stanley had invented a self-regulating d.c. dynamo and an incandescent lamp with a carbonized-silk filament. In 1884, H. H. Westinghouse introduced Stanley to George Westinghouse, who placed Stanley on the Union Switch and Signal Company staff with the intention of developing a complete incandescent-electric-lighting system based on Stanley's lamp and dynamo patents. These patents had been assigned to the Swan Incandescent Electric Light Company. Westinghouse purchased them for $50,-000. Stanley agreed to assign all future inventions to Westinghouse on the condition that Westinghouse make and sell them. Stanley was to receive one-tenth of the profits and a salary of $5,000 per year. Production of the lighting system was begun in 1884 by the Union Switch company. The Stanley lamps were exhibited at the Philadelphia Electric Exhibition in the fall of 1884. A number of lighting plants were installed in 1885 and 1886.

Westinghouse's interest in electric lighting prior to 1885 was not very strong, nor were his ideas unusual. He simply entered a field which he thought might be profitable. In the spring of 1885, however, his attention was drawn to a new method of transmitting electricity — with which he was to revolutionize the electrical industry. He read an article in an English engineering periodical which described an alternating-current system on display at the Inventions Exhibition in London. Gaulard and Gibbs transformers were used to change the voltage from a high transmission value to the low value necessary to operate incandescent lamps. The article described these "secondary generators" in great detail. It was stated that the induction coils had no moving parts, were 90 per cent efficient, and could be used to produce any desired voltage. Westinghouse began to see that alternating current, which could use the transformer, might provide an economical distribution system for electrical energy. . . .

In the summer of 1885, Westinghouse ordered several Gaulard and Gibbs transformers and a Siemens alternator from London. While awaiting the arrival of this equipment, he assigned Stanley and several other engineers to begin work on alternating current problems. The decision of Westinghouse to shift to alternating current was not in accord with the advice he received from his engineers and patent lawyers. [Guido] Pantaleoni [his employee] gave sole credit to Westinghouse for making the decision. "I investigated and reported on the Gaulard and Gibbs alternating current system . . . but the opposition by ALL the electric part of the Westinghouse organization was such that it was only Mr. George Westinghouse's personal will that put it through." "Generally the opposition was far greater than I had thought possible; George Westinghouse himself was the only man who was determined to go to the bottom of things."

. . . In summary, Westinghouse entered the electrical manufacturing industry in 1884 and produced a d.c. incandescent-lighting system. In 1886, it pioneered the first commercial a.c. incandescent-lighting system. In the years that followed, it merged with Consolidated, United States, and Waterhouse for the double purpose of strengthening its position in incandescent-lamp patents and adding arc-lighting equipment to its line of products.

* * *

Edison was a pioneer innovator whose contribution to economic development has been exceeded by very few persons. His work in mimeographs, telegraphy, stock tickers, phonographs, electrical equipment, telephones, storage batteries, and motion pictures — to mention only the more important fields in which he was an innovator — has been of enormous value to the world. With regard to his activities in the electrical industry, the most significant single statement that can be made is that, whatever his motivation, he set out to invent an electric-lighting system which would be commercially successful. He wanted to produce light with the smallest possible amount of resources. He realized that the meaningful test of inventive activities is economic. Can the product be made and sold at a price which will cover the cost of production? Unless his electric-lighting system passed that test, any claim that he benefited mankind would be open to question. The real meaning of the profit calculus in a market economy with consumers exercising freedom of choice can hardly be overemphasized. The word "profit" has been so frequently associated with income-distribution problems that the logic of profits has received very little attention. *Because* Edison's work was profit-oriented, not in spite of it, he fostered economic development, increased the national income, and raised the standard of living of the mass of the people. If he had refused to submit to the dictates of the profit calculus and market discipline and had acted instead in accord with some pattern of his own choosing, his contribution to human welfare would have been much smaller and perhaps nonexistent. If Edison had been motivated by broadly humanitarian ideals — and possibly he was — he could hardly have acted more effectively than he did.

How the pattern of Edison's activities in electric lighting was influenced by profit considerations can be briefly outlined. He chose electric lighting over other possible areas such as the telegraph, the telephone, and the phonograph because he felt that there were bigger rewards in lighting. In the electrical field, he was not interested in arc lighting or electric power. He believed that their profitability could not approach that of incandescent electric lighting. And in regard to the latter, he decided that he would have to set the price for light equivalent to the price of gas light. With the price thus fixed, the path to greatest profits was to reduce costs as much as possible. To lower costs, he made a series of inventions which were designed to economize the materials used in his incandescent-lighting system.

The economic orientation of Edison's inventive work in electric lighting defined his approach to the problem of subdividing the electric light. His goal was to invent a system which could produce light at the lowest possible cost. And his inventions were inventions primarily because he was looking for a low-cost lighting system. The Edison lamp differed from those that preceded it in the high resistance of its filament. Edison was the first inventor to realize that an incandescent lamp which could operate in a constant-voltage parallel circuit would necessarily have to be of high resistance in order to keep the cost of the copper conductors from being prohibitive. The high lamp resistance permitted a voltage high enough to reduce the copper cost to a reasonable level.

Edison's work in dynamo development was also directed toward reducing costs. His dynamo differed from those that preceded it in its high efficiency. He reduced the energy lost as heat in the dynamo by making the armature resistance as small as possible, by maintaining good contact between the pieces of iron in the magnetic circuit, and by using a very narrow gap between the armature and the pole pieces. Edison also attacked the waste of energy in transmission from the prime mover to the dynamo. His principal contribution here was to substitute a direct mechanical connection for the usual belt-pulley method.

The parallel between Edison's work on the dynamo and on the incandescent light is apparent. In each case, he perceived the function of the component in the system. He then determined the characteristic of that component which would result in a system with the lowest production cost of light. The next step was to apply the electrical principles and to conduct numerous experiments until the desired end was reached.

The transmission network which connected the dynamo and the lamps was a third main component of the Edison lighting system. As in the lamp and the dynamo, Edison's contribution was to invent a cost-reducing component. In his preliminary work on the lighting system, he had thought that an ordinary parallel network . . . would suffice. In this network, the lamps are of uneven illumination because the voltage is less on the lamps which are farther from the dynamo. One solution would be to construct lamps for operation on different voltages. The impossibility of controlling lamp voltages in manufacture and the complications which would arise in use of lamps of different voltages on a single circuit necessitated a change in the network. The object was to provide a uniform voltage for the lamps whether they were near or far from the dynamo; and the method was to use conductors of large cross-section near the dynamo, tapering off as the distance from the

dynamo increased. The large conductors prevented any appreciable voltage drop. The main drawback to this system was that a very large copper investment was required. When Upton had calculated that the amount of copper needed would cost about $25 per lamp, Edison realized that some means had to be found to reduce the copper cost. He finally evolved the feeder-main network. . . . The essence of this network was that the voltage drop took place in a feeder conductor. The main conductor could be operated at a nearly constant voltage. The amount of copper in the feeder could be determined with reference to minimizing the total of copper cost and energy loss and did not have to meet the problem of voltage variation at the individual lamps. The feeder system cut copper costs by about 85 per cent. Calculations made at an infringement trial involving the feeder patent showed that it reduced copper investment for an area of nine city blocks containing 8,640 lamps from $200,000 to $30,000 (with copper at $0.25 per pound).

The Pearl Street station in New York City used the two-wire feeder network, but Edison sought to lessen the cost of copper still further. Early in 1883, he invented the three-wire system. . . . This reduced the copper to approximately what would be required if the potential difference across each light were increased from 110 volts to 220 volts. The outside conductors could consequently be cut to one-fourth their previous size. Because the use of the third, balancing wire added some copper, the net saving over the two-wire system was not 75 per cent but only 63 per cent. The main advantage of the three-wire principle, like the feeder-main principle, was that it saved copper without raising the voltage on the individual lamps. The two inventions together reduced the copper cost per lamp from the original $25 to less than $1.50.

The fourth main component of the Edison lighting system — the meter — was also a cost-reducing invention, but not in the same sense that the other three were. The lamp, the dynamo, and the distribution network were designed to form a lighting system which would, for a given amount of light, use the smallest amount of resources. The meter was designed to inform the light company and the consumer how much light the consumer was using. The light company could thereby charge the consumer in accordance with the cost of producing the light he used. The consumer was encouraged to use light only for those purposes which he felt justified the expenditure. He was given an incentive to economize in the use of light just as he would in the usual economic good. The result was that the same number of customers could be served with lower operating expenses and a smaller investment in generating and transmission equipment than if meters were not used. The cost of light per consumer was therefore less, and, at the same time, the consumers were using light only where its utility to them was great enough to justify its cost. The meter, in short, economized not by reducing the amount of resources needed to produce a given quantity of light — that is, by reducing "waste" in production — but by reducing the amount of light consumed — that is, by reducing "waste" in consumption. If a product is treated by consumers as though it were a free good, the total production costs can conceivably be so high that it is impossible to cover them. Consumption waste can stand in the way of commercial success just as production waste can. Edison's meter was similar to

the other three components. It economized the scarce resources of society.

The significance of Edison's work in electric lighting should by now be apparent. It was not his contributions to science, although he understood scientific laws better than many scientists of his day. It was not his inventive work, although he is probably one of the most ingenious, thorough, and painstaking inventors the world has ever known. It was not his engineering work, although he excelled in the design and construction of simple, reliable, and practical lighting systems. Edison's significance is the economic value of his scientific, inventive, and engineering activities. Everything he did was directed by the realization that, in a free economic society, the market test is the sole test of achievement. If the result of a man's work can command the purchasing power of the consumers in a free market, that work is worth doing.

The following statement by Edison summarizes the point of view that is mainly responsible for his achievements:

Clarke, Doctor ——— is a fine fellow. He knows a lot but he doesn't stick to the job. I set him at work developing details of a plan. But when he happens to note some phenomenon new to him, though easily seen to be of no importance in this apparatus, he gets sidetracked, follows it up and loses time. *We can't be spending time that way!* We have got to keep working up things of commercial value — that is what this laboratory is for. We can't be like the old German professor who as long as he can get his black bread and beer is content to spend his whole life studying the fuzz on a bee!

. . . The innovational work of Edison in electric lighting can be more adequately judged if a comparison is made with his contemporary inventors who failed to innovate. The incandescent-light inventors, with the exception of Edison, either did not envision the place that electric lighting could occupy and therefore could not design a practical system or they lacked the technical ability to invent such a system. All but one of the unsuccessful inventors, as far as can be determined, fall into the former category. These inventors sought a durable lamp of low resistance. Such a lamp could not be part of a commercial system, because if the lamps were connected in parallel, the copper cost would be prohibitive. If they were connected in series, independent control would have been possible only with heavy expense and undue complication. Various of the inventors had one or more of Edison's ideas, but none had them all. Sawyer worked with parallel circuits, but insisted on low-resistance lamps. He believed that resistance was a characteristic to be avoided. Swan, an English inventor and the man whom the English people believed to have invented the incandescent electric light, did excellent work on incandescent materials, but the resistance of his lamps was low and he advocated the series system. Furthermore, he made no attempt to develop the other components needed in a complete lighting system. Maxim produced only low-resistance lamps until after Edison had announced his high-resistance unit. The only inventor who, like Edison, had the concept of a system using high-resistance lamps connected in parallel was an English inventor, Lane-Fox. But he was unable to make a workable high-resistance filament.

Edison's innovational abilities were largely confined to the sphere of technical activity. In business administration and in marketing, he usually employed methods which were already in use. It has been shown that he closely imitated the gas companies in the business practices of his first commercial central station. The forming of that first illuminating company might be labeled an act of innovation, but it will be recalled that Brush promoted arc-lighting central stations as early as 1879. Likewise, Edison's formation of the first three-wire central stations, which were entirely owned by him, followed a precedent set several years earlier by Goff. Edison apparently believed that the marketing methods and the techniques of business organization and administration that had been developed by the gas industry and the arc-lighting industry were adequate for his purposes.

The fact that Edison did not innovate except in technology can also be attributed to the lack of any time for nontechnical innovation. Research, inventing, and manufacturing kept him fully occupied until about 1885. He was ultimately responsible for operation of the Menlo Park laboratory, the various manufacturing companies, and the Pearl Street station. There is little evidence that he succeeded in delegating much of the entrepreneurial function. He had well-trained assistants who were capable and trustworthy, but he alone had the full vision and complete technical understanding of his lighting system, and he had to give continual attention to the activities of his various enterprises. One exception may have been S. J. Bergmann, who operated the accessories-manufacturing plant very ably. He received the least direction from Edison, although the products made had to be capable of use with the Edison system. In the absence of assistants with the initiative and business acumen of Bergmann, Edison was almost solely responsible for the design, manufacture, sale, and installation of his lighting system. When he began to withdraw from his electrical activities, after 1885, the Edison companies suffered from the lack of an imaginative and decisive leader. The difficulty was not corrected until the consolidation with Thomson-Houston in 1892. Coffin then supplied the leadership that was needed.

After the Edison system had been in operation for several years, it became apparent that the heavy copper investment required by the low-voltage distribution system severely limited the area that one central station could serve. The result was that the cost of electric lighting was high, and none but the upper-income classes could use it freely. Furthermore, electric lighting was restricted to areas of dense population. If a low-cost distribution system were available, the area served by one central station could be increased with resulting generation economies, and it would be economic to serve districts of low consumer density. Many inventors knew that a low-cost distribution system was needed and that high voltages would reduce copper costs substantially. But no one was able to devise a satisfactory high-voltage system. If it were a series system, it brought high voltage into the home and made independent control of lights difficult. If the battery were used as a voltage converter, the system was unreliable and inefficient. Westinghouse was among those who realized that the use of electric lighting was being retarded by high transmission costs. His experience with natural gas had taught him that the solution could be a system which used high voltage for transmission and converted it into low voltage at the point of use. When he heard of the Gaulard and Gibbs transformers, he realized that they might be the conversion device he was looking for. With an

able group of engineers, he designed a complete alternating-current system. The main technical contributions of Westinghouse and his staff were the designing of an efficient, inexpensive, and reliable transformer, connecting these transformers in parallel, developing an efficient alternator, and inventing an alternating-current meter. Westinghouse left undisturbed the basic features of the Edison system — the parallel connection of lamps and the central-station method — and improved the major weakness, the high cost of distribution.

* * *

The similarity between the two pioneer innovators in incandescent lighting, Edison and Westinghouse, is striking. Both borrowed techniques from the gas industry. Both set out to develop an entire system, and both took a personal interest in the invention of the system components. The impetus behind the principal inventions in each system was to reduce costs. Edison found a parallel in the gas system, which served as his guide. Westinghouse found a parallel in the d.c. incandescent system, which served as his guide. Edison formed a number of firms to manufacture the components of his system. Westinghouse formed a firm to manufacture the components of his system. And both Edison and Westinghouse had become famous as inventors in other fields before turning to the problems of incandescent lighting.

The most important similarity between Edison and Westinghouse is the doggedness, the perseverance, and the faith in his own ideas that each possessed. Thomson and Coffin did not seem to have any of these qualities to the same degree. It is probable that a pioneer innovator must possess these qualities or he never could complete his work. Both Edison and Westinghouse ran into strong resistance when they attempted to carry out their plans.

The official biographers of Edison report that he never saw a statement in a scientific book without involuntarily challenging it and wishing to demonstrate that it was either right or wrong. He was an independent thinker and took nothing on authority. The interesting aspect of such a person is that once he is convinced he is right, he cannot be shaken. This rule applies to cases where Edison, in fact, was right and where, in fact, he was wrong. In his work on lighting, he sought to subdivide the electric light, a goal which many scientists thought impossible. He designed a generator with as low an internal resistance as possible and was labeled by some engineers as incompetent. His plan of a central-station lighting system was believed by many to have no chance of success. In all these things, Edison was right. But in some other projects, he was completely wrong. His opposition to alternating current is a good example. He refused to admit its utility and would not relinquish his belief. Another belief he held was that electricity could be produced directly from coal, just as electricity is produced in a primary battery by the consumption of zinc. He hoped thus to eliminate the 70 per cent energy loss caused by the steam engine. He worked on this problem for many years. In 1884, he announced, "I have got far enough to know the thing is possible. I can get quite a current now directly from the combustion of fuel." He thought that he could achieve his objective in five years. That Edison really considered electricity direct from coal as a probable development is proved by the fact that the patent-license contracts between Edison General Electric and the Edison licensees covered all equipment to be used for the generation of electricity except that which was produced directly from coal. How much money Edison spent on coal research is not known, but it was probably substantial. Edison had other ideas which in the eyes of modern scientists are not worth pursuing. Shortly before his death in 1931, he expressed the belief that an alloy could be found which would insulate from gravity.

Westinghouse was also an independent thinker and had the courage to act on his beliefs no matter how strong the opposition. When he brought out his alternating-current system, he was opposed by Edison, the most famous inventor and electrician of that day, and by Thomson, a highly respected engineer. As the a.c.-d.c. controversy progressed, Westinghouse became subject to more and more violent attacks and abuse. But he held his ground because he believed that he was right, and, before very long, the purchasers of electrical equipment vindicated his viewpoint. Westinghouse was right when he believed alternating current was superior to direct current for the transmission of electrical energy. Westinghouse was also right some years earlier when he proved that a certain accepted law of friction was wrong. In a series of air-brake tests carried out in England in 1878–79, he demonstrated that friction sometimes varies inversely as the velocity and is not always independent of it, as had been stated in a certain "law of nature."

Westinghouse, like Edison, could be wrong, but he, too, refused to accept other people's judgments. This was shown when an early paper by Lord Kelvin on thermodynamics came to his attention. The paper stimulated his imagination, and after considerable thought he drew up plans for a device which would use the heat of the atmosphere to generate power. When he submitted these plans to Lord Kelvin, the English physicist told Westinghouse that such a device could not possibly work. Engineers in the Westinghouse organization told him the same thing. But he continued until nearly the end of his life trying to devise an atmospheric engine which was, in reality, a perpetual-motion machine. Westinghouse had known laws of nature and great authorities to be wrong before. He refused to give up his project until convinced by his own experiments.

Thomas W. Lawson: PIONEERS AND SPECULATORS — WESTINGHOUSE VERSUS "THE SYSTEM"

Thomas W. Lawson (1857–1925), a remarkable Boston speculator who had made over $10,000,000 on the Exchange before he was thirty, wrote a dramatic public revelation of stock-watering techniques in Everybody's *in 1904 and doubled that magazine's circulation in a few months, not ceasing to speculate himself throughout the entire transaction. His articles took book form as* Frenzied Finance *in 1905 — a classic muckraking work.*

Even in the highly technical electrical industry "Robber Baron" activity was still possible; but in the following short chapter from Lawson's book the author dissociates George Westinghouse from such behavior, and portrays him as an honest scientific pioneer, struggling against the "System" of Wall Street speculators.

IN 1894 I had just wound up one of the most strenuous and successful financial campaigns I ever engaged in. This was the Westinghouse deal, of which the papers were full at the time. George Westinghouse, to whom the world owes the air-brake and countless improvements in electrical machinery, having surmounted the difficulties that clog the early steps of the inventor who would be his own master, had taken rank, some years before, among the prominent public figures of the day. The various corporations in America bearing his name had prospered amazingly; his ingenious appliances had displaced home products in the European market; and titles and decorations had been conferred on the inventor, though these last, like the sturdy American he is, Westinghouse had put aside.

This great success was wholly the fruit of George Westinghouse's personal endeavor. It owed nothing to extraneous influences. It had been accomplished along those manly, independent, Yankee lines which have made that name synonymous with hustle and success in every part of the civilized world. Above all, the man had organized and developed his companies without the aid of the "System" or without truckling to its

From Thomas W. Lawson, *Frenzied Finance: The Crime of Amalgamated* (New York, 1905).

votaries. In consequence he had incurred the deadly hatred of some of its lords paramount.

In the business world Westinghouse's great rival was the General Electric Company. To mention "Westinghouse" and "General Electric" in the same breath was to speak of a thing and its antithesis. Everything George Westinghouse was or had been the General Electric was not and had never been. The General Electric had been and was by leave of the "System"; in fact, was one of the very foremost examples of its methods. Its high-priest was J. Pierpont Morgan; its home, Wall Street; its owners, the principal votaries of the "System." It had grown because of their favor and by means of the rankest exhibitions of knock-down-and-drag-out methods of consolidation of all competitors but — Westinghouse.

Just previous to 1894 Westinghouse had rejected a dazzling scheme of uniting the two institutions on an immense capitalization which would have absorbed millions and millions of the people's savings and earned millions in commissions for its projectors. Wall Street's indignation at his hardihood knew no bounds, and at the time of which I write the yegg-men of the "System" were laying for him with dark-lantern and sand-bag.

To appreciate the story of what the "System" tried to do to George Westinghouse and what he withstood, one must know the man. He embodies in many ways the conception of what the ideal American should be. His remarkable six feet and odd of physique and his fertile, powerful brain are the admiration of all true men with whom he comes in contact. In spite of his unparalleled success and the accumulation of a great fortune, he retains the same simplicity of manner and conduct that characterized him when working at the bench for weekly wages, and with all his shrewdness and force of character he has preserved a simple, honest, childlike belief in humanity. Single-handed he conducted all his great enterprises on a plain, patriarchal basis, using their revenues for extensions, and depending on his faithful and well-satisfied stockholders for such further accessions of capital as the business might in his judgment need. About the time General Electric was most anxious to bolster up its jerry-built structure with the solid Westinghouse concern, the latter institution had begun the erection of some big new plants which required immediately several millions additional capital. Westinghouse prepared to apply to his stockholders for the required funds, and the announcement was to be made at the annual election soon due. Suddenly the financial sky became overcast. The stock-market grew panicky and money as scarce in Wall Street as rain in Arizona in May. It was just such a situation as the "System" might have brought about to accomplish its fell designs had it possessed the power to work miracles.

And the "System" took care of its advantage. At a tense moment in that soul and nerve trying period, with Wall and State streets full of talk about General Electric's probable absorption of Westinghouse, General Electric being then at its highest price, $119 per share, the Westinghouse companies held their annual meetings and the big inventor, confidently facing his stockholders, quite regardless of conditions which he thought could have no possible bearing on his concern's splendid prospects, came forward with his demand for the millions required to complete the projects already under way. This was the signal. From all the stock-market sub-cellars and rat-holes of State, Broad, and Wall streets crept those wriggling, slimy snakes of bastard rumors which, seemingly fatherless and motherless, have in reality multi-parents who beget them with a deviltry of intention: "George Westinghouse had mismanaged his companies"; "George Westinghouse, because of gross extravagance, had spread himself and his companies until they were involved beyond extrication unless by consolidation with General Electric"; these and many more seeped through the financial haunts of Boston, Philadelphia, and New York, and kept hot the wires into every financial centre in America and Europe, where aid must be sought to relieve the crisis. There came a crash in Westinghouse stocks, and their price melted. From amidst the thunder and lowering clouds emerged the "System." "Notwithstanding the black eye the name of everything Westinghouse had received, it would stand by and consolidate and save the day!" But the "System" and its everything-gauged-by-machinery votaries had reckoned without their host. George Westinghouse was too strong a man to be thus easily shaken down. He threw back his mighty shoulders, shook his big head, and flung his great private fortune into the market to stay the falling prices of his securities. The movement was too strong against him at the moment, and his millions were but a temporary help. He got on the firing-line himself and did a thousand and one things that only a brave, honest, and democratic Yankee would or could do — everything but accept the cunning aid offered him by the "System" or its votaries. He knew too well that the friendly mask concealed a foe and that the kid-gloved hand extended him had a dagger up its sleeve.

These were the conditions when I, as an expert in stock-market affairs, was called in for assistance. Here was this sound, sturdy institution standing for everything that was best and self-supporting in American finance adrift on the Wall Street shoals, and it seemed almost a hopeless task to attempt its rescue. But it was a task eminently worth while, and I undertook it with all the energy I could command.

The problem was to restore the Westinghouse stocks to their former high price, and, confidence being re-established, to sell the new treasury stock at such a figure as would pay for the plants and other projects the company had under way. The completion of these meant greatly increased earnings and such an advance in facilities and economy of manufacture as would surely seal the fate of General Electric if it competed with Westinghouse under the new conditions. Small wonder "Standard Oil's" whole strength was bent to force the alliance.

My fight had hardly begun when I saw it was to be opposed by all the forces of General Electric and the "System," and I concluded defeat was sure unless by a counter movement on their stock I could keep them so busy that they would have no time to interfere with Westinghouse. Thereupon I laid out that attack on everything connected with General Electric which created so much consternation at the time. To this day, if my enemies are asked to name the act which most conclusively justifies their hatred of me, they will point to my terrible General Electric raid. They will tell you I broke the stock from 118 to 56 in a day, and thereby caused one of our most disastrous panics; that I continued to hammer it to 20, that I compelled reorganization, and then did not let up. They will show you that the misery and ruin I wrought were beyond calculation. I will only say that, of any of the things I am proud of having done, I am proudest of what I did in General Electric, and, willingly, I would give over five years of my life to go through the experience again.

It was a most arduous campaign, and our fate trembled many times in the balance. By dint of hard, overtime work, and what my enemies were pleased to call rank manipulation, we drove Westinghouse stock back to its former price, after which a strong syndicate was formed to take the new stock, and the righted institution at once magnificently swept on its international career which to-day is at its height.

Though I had taken up the Westinghouse cause as a business venture and its successful termination was most profitable to me, I had entered into the campaign with the ardor of a lawyer defending a client unjustly accused of a heinous crime. But there was this difference — if in spite of his efforts the lawyer fails to convince the jury of his client's innocence it means no detriment to his fortune or his reputation, whereas all I had and was were involved in this stock-exchange struggle. The great rewards that are the guerdon of success in financial fights are balanced by the terrific consequences of defeat. The broker general engaged in surrounding his enemy requires every dollar he and his principals can pledge or beg, and where great forces are in conflict millions are burnt up to seize any vantage, as Kuroki sacrifices a regiment to gain a hill. I had won for myself as well as for Westinghouse, but if the fortunes of the war had been on the other side, I must certainly have been wiped out.

V. THE CONTROVERSY RESTATED BY RECENT OBSERVERS

Allen Solganick: PIRATES

The youngest scholar represented in this book, Allen Solganick (1941–   ), is by training an economist; but he has a lively and critical interest in economic history, as this exposé of the Robber Barons reveals. He is assistant professor of economics at San Jose State College, California, where he is engaged in research on problems of planning and the market in socialist economies. In this forthright article, he questions not only the alleged achievements of the Robber Barons, but also those of the United States economy as a whole. A major defense of the business leaders was their contribution to rapid economic growth in the late nineteenth century. But Mr. Solganick, with his knowledge of non-capitalist experiences, questions that growth record itself.

CONCOMITANT with the development of the Cold War has been the rise of a self-proclaimed school of revisionist historians who purport to improve our understanding of American economic history in the period between the Civil War and the turn of the century. Specifically, they feel that the Robber Baron concept of business enterprise is in need of substantial revision. The individual historians in this school hold diverse opinions as to several aspects of the Robber Barons' activities, but are unanimous in agreeing that big businessmen played a creative role in the development of the American economy. Indeed, this creativity is the unifying theme of the revisionist school. H. Wayne Morgan states the revisionist argument thusly: "Suffice it to say that the stereotype of the Robber Baron is much overdrawn. It must be balanced with a fuller picture, showing the new technology he often brought to his industry, the wealth and resources he developed for the economy in general, the social good he sometimes did with his money offsetting the bitter fact that he paid little taxes."

This "stereotype" of which Morgan speaks has been developed by men like Gustavus Myers, Thorstein Veblen, and Matthew Josephson. Chronicling the careers of men of wealth in the United States, Myers showed the use of government and extra-legal methods in the accumulation of private fortunes. His work was largely ignored until Josephson resurrected it in the 1930's when business came under general attack. Josephson drew not only on the work of Myers and the "muckrakers," but also on the theoretical contributions of Veblen who asserted that although some capitalists had played a creative role with respect to technology and economic growth prior to 1860, after that time they became a

From Allen Solganick, "The Robber Baron Concept and Its Revisionists," *Science and Society* (Summer, 1965), Vol. XXIX, No. 3. Reprinted by permission of the publishers and author, with omission of some footnotes.

drag on development, administering "a salutary running margin of sabotage in production, at the cost of the underlying population."

The present paper is both a rebuttal of recent revisionist work and a revindication of Veblen's view. The first part discusses attempts by the revisionists to discredit the critics of monopoly, and the attempts to portray the era as one during which everyone was satisfied. The second section deals with the question of monopoly. Finally, the matter of whether the Robber Barons were in fact creative with respect to technology and economic growth is handled in the third section.

THE ROBBER BARONS, THE CRITICS AND DISCONTENT

As one basis for the need for a fresh look at American capitalism, the revisionists have attempted to discredit various critics of monopoly. Thus, one writer bewails the "anti-capitalist bias" of American historians. Another entitled his article "The Anatomy of Prejudice: Origins of the Robber Baron Legend." Still another concluded that the Robber Baron concept was "born apparently of a desire for denunciation rather than objective analysis." And, "no recent student approached the era with more bias than did Matthew Josephson, three of whose works have remained standard interpretations of the period for a generation."[1]

One is prompted to ask how Josephson's work managed such general acceptance if he was so evidently biased? However, a more important question is what evidence of "bias," "prejudice," and "non-objectivity" have the above quoted authors brought forth? The answer, of course, is none; the sole basis of their charges is not that the facts were dishonestly reported, but rather that the critics were guilty of misinterpreting those facts. This assertion by the revisionists is in turn based on their assumption that the Robber Barons were creative, a matter to be dealt with later.

Professor Kirkland, on the other hand, actually claims to have discovered distortion of evidence by Henry Demarest Lloyd, author of the famous *Wealth Against Commonwealth*. Dubbing it a "utopian fantasy," Kirkland goes on to state that charges in Lloyd's book "had the paraphernalia of documentation and footnote reference," but "the handling of evidence is not persuasive." The only example of distortion which is given by Kirkland is a misinterpretation of the connection between Standard Oil and the Rothschilds.[2] Yet, Professor C. M. Destler, writing fifteen years prior to the publication of Kirkland's book, found that in checking 420 of Lloyd's 648 references to source material only 10 inaccuracies in statement occurred, and these in ways "not of great import." Of 241 important undocumented statements, 229 were verified completely, 8 partially, and only 4 were incorrect. Destler was forced to conclude that "when all allowances are made, Lloyd's pioneering report of

---

[1] In sequence, these quotations come from L. M. Hacker, "The Anti-Capitalist Bias of American Historians," in *Capitalism and the Historians*, ed. F. A. Hayek (Chicago, 1954), pp. 64–92; John Tipple, "The Anatomy of Prejudice, Origins of the Robber Baron Legend," *Business History Review*, XXXIII, Winter, 1959, pp. 511–524; H. Bridges, "The Robber Baron Concept in American History," *Business History Review*, XXXII, Spring, 1958, pp. 1–13; H. Wayne Morgan, *The Gilded Age: A Reappraisal*, p. 5. For similar expressions see the articles by Fritz Redlich, *American Journal of Economics and Sociology*,

XII, January, 1953, pp. 163–177, and W. Woodruff, "History and the Businessman," *Business History Review*, XXX, September, 1956, pp. 241–259.

[2] *Industry Comes of Age* (New York, 1961), pp. 306–308.

the methods by which the oil monopoly was established and maintained remains substantially unaltered. . . .".[3] Hence, Professor Kirkland can be the only scholar to whom Lloyd's evidence is "not persuasive." The attempts to discredit these Robber Baron historians as being irrational, compulsive denouncers (Bridges), most biased (Morgan), pseudo-scientific and unscholarly (Kirkland), turns out to be biased on assertion only. That is, it is entirely unsubstantiated. The Robber Baron school of historians bases its criticisms of big business on solid documentation of the facts. This leaves the revisionists with only one criticism left. Namely, that the Robber Baron school presented only one side of the picture, leaving out the positive contribution made by the big businessmen. As will be shown later, this criticism is also based on assertion only.

However, the revisionists do not depend solely on discrediting critics of monopoly. They claim that this era was one of general satisfaction among the populace. Kirkland argues that if business were indeed greedy, without social purpose, dishonest, and exploitative, the "Republican Party, the party of big business," would not have "enjoyed almost uninterrupted political success. . . . Perhaps it is simpler to believe that the performance of the economy during this era was not as bad as pictured and in general won popular endorsement."[4] Furthermore, he contends that the statement that the rich got richer and the poor poorer is "completely inaccurate."[5]

These arguments are quite incorrect. Simon Kuznets found increasing inequal-

ity of income occurring during the period between 1870 and 1900, primarily due to the trust movement which resulted in substantial capital gains to those who were already rich.[6] Kirkland is right if he is speaking of absolute income levels. However, it would be correct to say that during this period the rich were getting richer and the poor relatively poorer. As many economists have shown, relative rather than absolute income is more important for the individual's comparisons with other people. Marx pointed out that "although the enjoyments of the worker have risen, the social satisfaction that they give has fallen in comparison with the increased enjoyments of the capitalists, which are inaccessible to the worker, in comparison with the state of development of society in general."[7]

In reply to the argument that the recurrent election of Republicans indicated a general contentment with business, it should be noted that both parties were "parties of big business." Corruption was quite widespread, and as two of Kirkland's fellow revisionists have pointed out, whenever discontented groups fought for reforms "they met the disciplined representatives of the ruling cliques, who had sufficient resources to beat almost any candidate, platform plank, or bill they disliked. The improvised organizations of the protestants could not compete with the major parties. . . . Mute testimony to the failure of groups outside the ruling interests lies in the Republican and Democratic platforms; the record of Republican and Democratic administrations tells that

[3] *American Radicalism,* 1865–1891 (New London, Conn., 1946), pp. 144, 146.
[4] "The Robber Barons Revisited," *American Historical Review,* LXVI (October, 1960), pp. 68–73.
[5] *Industry Comes of Age,* p. 405.

[6] "Proportion of Capital Formation to National Product," *American Economic Review,* XLII (May, 1952), pp. 522–523.
[7] "Wage-Labour and Capital," in *Selected Works* (New York, 1935), Vol. I, p. 269. In current literature on the consumption function this phenomenon is called the "Veblen effect," based on Veblen's discussions of "invidious comparisons."

failure aloud."[8] Many factors are necessary to explain the Republican ascendancy, and to claim a lack of discontent as the primary reason is clearly untrue.

There are no indexes available showing the rise and fall of popular discontent, but if one could be constructed it would undoubtedly exhibit a steadily upward trend during the Gilded Age. This was an era which witnessed the birth of the Grangers, Greenbackers, Populists, National Labor Union, A. F. L., and numerous other groups of discontented citizens. Indeed, it was the farmers of Kansas who first used the term "Robber Baron" to describe railroad leaders in an anti-monopoly pamphlet written in 1880. One populist song of the period spoke of "monopolies banded together to beat a poor hayseed like me," while labor added to the refrain that "those mean monopolizers had the cheek to take the stand, and ask to get protection from the honest working man."[9]

The famous incidents of discontent, like Homestead and Pullman, are reflected in the high level of aggregate strike activity during this period. Work stoppages which, for the five-year period 1881–1885, averaged 528 per year and involved an annual average of 176,000 workers, increased with fluctuations so that the corresponding figures for the period 1896–1900 were 1390 and 386,-000.[10] During a period characterized by a high degree of instability, with major downturns in 1872, 1882, and 1892, discontent should be expected. The per-centage decline in output of consumer durables for the cycles of 1872, 1882, and 1892 were respectively 33, 25, and 34. Of the total of 35 years between 1865 and 1900, 16 were depression years.[11] One author estimated average unemployment in the period 1889–1898 to be twelve per cent of the total labor force.[12] However, even when they were employed, workers had reason for discontent. The number of deaths and injuries of employees on railroads for the 1890's was enormous. In 1900 there were 1,018,000 railroad workers employed of whom 2,550 were killed and 39,643 injured that year. By contrast, in 1957 with a work force almost exactly the same size, the number of deaths and injuries on the job declined to 195 and 12,245 respectively.[13] Thus, working conditions must have been very hazardous if railroad conditions are any indication.

Professor Kirkland's argument that discontent was infrequent has no basis in fact. The Robber Baron, John D. Rockefeller, was certainly not speaking of a docile working class when he wrote in 1907 that "these stories about my wealth. They have a bad effect on a class of people with whom it is becoming difficult to deal . . . the stress which is laid in those stories arouses hatred and envy not against the individual only but against organized society. . . . It is the general trend I have in mind, which is arraying the masses against the classes."

THE ROBBER BARONS AND MONOPOLY

The concentration movement in American industry after the Civil War is a well-known fact. Alfred Chandler found

[8] Thomas C. Cochran and William Miller, *The Age of Enterprise*, p. 165.

[9] The songs are respectively from Anna Rochester, *The Populist Movement in the United States* (New York, 1943), p. 2, and John Greenway, *American Folksongs of Protest* (New York, 1960), p. 53.

[10] Calculated from United States Bureau of the Census, *Historical Statistics of the United States: Colonial Times to 1957* (Washington, D. C., 1960), p. 99.

[11] Alvin Hansen, *Business Cycles and National Income* (New York, 1951), pp. 24, 26–28.

[12] Simon Kuznets, "Proportion of Capital Formation to National Product," *op. cit.*, p. 523.

[13] United States Bureau of the Census, *Historical Statistics*, p. 437.

that when continued production at full capacity threatened to drop prices to the detriment of profits, "many small manufacturers in the leather, sugar, salt, distilling and other corn products, linseed and cotton oil, biscuit, petroleum, fertilizer, and rubber boot and glove industries joined in large horizontal combinations. In most of these industries, combination was followed by consolidation and vertical integration, and the pattern was comparatively consistent."[14] However, the revisionists deny that this meant monopoly was spreading. For instance, Kirkland states that "though combinations were often bewailed by critics as likely to lead to the imposition of 'extortionate' and 'monopoly' rates, the large corporations were precisely those which were most enterprising in the adoption of cost saving devices."[15]

Whether the large corporations were in fact "the most enterprising" in technological innovation will be the subject of the next section. The question here is, to the extent that costs were lowered by large corporations, how much of this meant higher monopoly profits and how much benefit did the consumer experience? The simple fact of an adoption of cost-saving equipment tells us nothing about who were the beneficiaries. Nor can the citation of price reductions tell us whether or not monopoly power was exerted, for this period witnessed about a 25 per cent decline in the general level of prices.[16]

On the other hand, much evidence exists which confirms the generally accepted view that this was a period when monopoly became a major element in the economic and political life of the nation. One noted economist has succinctly stated why combinations occurred at this time: "Competition is profit-destroying and monopoly is profit preserving. Consequently profit-motivated economic units attempted to establish monopolies whenever possible."[17] That this maxim applied to the Robber Barons has been confirmed several times.

The Hepburn Committee in 1879 found that 90 per cent to 95 per cent of all the refiners in the country acted in harmony with Standard Oil and in 1892 the Supreme Court of Ohio declared that the object of the Standard Oil Company was "to establish a virtual monopoly of the business of producing petroleum, and of manufacturing, refining and dealing in it and all its products throughout the entire country, and by which it might not merely control the production, but the price, at its pleasure."

The example of Standard Oil is multiplied in the aggregate. It was the belief of the Industrial Commission in 1902, after a most exhaustive study, "that in most cases the combination has exerted an appreciable power over prices and in practically all cases it has increased the margin between raw materials and finished products. Since there is reason to believe that the cost of production over a period of years has lessened, the conclusion is inevitable that the combinations have been able to increase their profits." In addition, while monopolies had presumably been banned under the common law, 27 states and territories by the close of 1890 had seen fit to pass laws intended to prevent or destroy them.

The most important study of the relationship of the Robber Baron to monopoly was done by Pofessor C. M. Destler,

14 "The Beginnings of 'Big Business' in American Industry," *Business History Review*, XXXIII, Spring, 1959, pp. 1–31, 343–344.

15 *Industry Comes of Age*, p. 96.

16 United States Bureau of the Census, *Historical Statistics*, p. 127.

17 Dudley Dillard, "Capitalism after 1850," in *Chapters in Western Civilization* (New York, 1960), p. 279.

who studied 43 notable capitalists of this
era.[18] He found that 16 had milked their
corporations for their own profit; 23
charged exorbitant rates when a monopoly position made it possible; 13 profited
from control and manipulation of the
press; at least 13 practiced political corruption; 16 exhibited marked hostility to
the labor movement; and railroad favors
in rates or services were important for 11.
He was forced to conclude that "monopoly, partially or wholly, temporarily or
more permanently achieved, was a significant or dominant feature of the entrepreneurial activity of at least thirty-six of
the forty-three."

Destler was convinced by his study
that "for the bulk of the entrepreneurs
studied and for many other contemporary business leaders, there is justification [for the term] 'the robber barons,'
or Howard Mumford Jones' analogy with
the Renaissance despot. . . ." His view is
shared by two more recent writers who,
while still clinging to the belief that the
Robber Barons played a creative role,
nevertheless condemn their more piratical aspects. Thus, Tipple states that "if
big businessmen like John D. Rockefeller
were attacked as Robber Barons, it was
because they were correctly identified as
destroyers." And Miller asserts that "the
Progressive indictment survives in the
general history books because it is a true
bill." All of the available evidence points
up the fact that this era witnessed the
emergence of large-scale monopoly, and
no facts have been advanced which
would modify this view.

THE ROBBER BARONS' ALLEGED CREATIVITY

The theme which unifies the revisionist school is that, regardless of any cupid-

ity, no one can deny the fact that the
Robber Barons played *the* creative role
in the economic development of the
country. For example, a recent textbook
asserts that "without business leadership,
no amounts of capital, natural resources,
or labor could have brought the United
States into its position of industrial pre-
dominance." Another author notes a
"striking growth of output." Still another
states that the system at this time "added
immensely to both natural and human
wealth." A much used source book on
this period speaks of "decades of prodigious expansion," and Professor Kirkland
claims that the talent for business enterprise was "the source of abundance." The
progressive Professor Tipple states that
this was "an age when the corporation
made unprecedented achievements in
production." And finally, even William
Appleman Williams, who otherwise is in
no way connected with the revisionists,
speaks of a "tremendous surge of industrial strength" which is "the undeniable
achievement of the laissez-faire entrepreneur. . . ."[19]

The use of words such as "striking,"
"immensely," "prodigious," "abundance,"
"unprecedented," and "tremendous"
would lead one to believe that the record
of growth was noteworthy, to say the
least. However, the facts do not warrant
such a conclusion, whether we compare
the performance of the economy with
previous performance, with the performance of other capitalist economies either

[18] "Entrepreneurial Leadership Among the
Robber Barons: A Trial Balance," *The Tasks of
Economic History*, Supplement VI of the *Journal
of Economic History*, 1946, pp. 28–49.

[19] In sequence, these quotations come from G. C.
Fite and J. E. Reese, *An Economic History of the
United States* (New York, 1964), p. 350; J. A.
Schumpeter, *Capitalism, Socialism, and Democ-
racy* (New York, 1962), p. 107; William Miller,
A New History of the United States (New York,
1958), p. 269; Thomas C. Cochran and William
Miller, *The Age of Enterprise*, p. 249; E. C. Kirk-
land, *Industry Comes of Age*, p. 408; John Tipple,
"The Robber Baron in the Gilded Age," p. 33;
and W. A. Williams, *The Contours of American
History* (New York, 1961), p. 325.

during the same period or at a later date, or with the performance of the socialist economies. Indeed, as will be shown below, "the depression of 1893–1896 was the culmination of more than two decades of unsatisfactory performance of the American economy."[20]

Since investment in fixed capital is an important determinant of growth, we would expect a very high growth rate in the post-Civil War era. Instead, we find that the average decennial rate of growth of fixed capital was much higher during the period 1839–1859 than it was in 1869–1899.[21] Thus, in comparison with earlier achievements in the growth of fixed capital, the United States witnessed a decline, not a "surge."

Another indicator in judging growth is the output of commodities. Since services were not a very significant factor during this period, the commodity output figures are a close approximation to total income. Not only was the average decennial rate of change of value added in agriculture, mining, and construction lower in the post-Civil War period, but this was also true of manufacturing, supposedly the area where "fantastic" and "prodigious" rates of growth were to be found. It is difficult to reconcile the assertions of the revisionists with the actual facts. The evidence shows that the United States developed more slowly during the era of the Robber Barons than it had before these "creators" arrived on the scene.

Not only does the United States during this period exhibit an unspectacular record with regard to its own past, but also three other countries, Sweden, Denmark, and Canada, were experiencing the same rate of growth of per capita income.[22]

And, of course, many capitalist countries have displayed higher growth rates than this in the twentieth century. Finally, when we compare the United States' record of about four per cent a year increase in Gross National Product with the nine per cent a year figure which is a conservative estimate of China's growth, the record does not seem so striking."[23]

Relating to this "surge" of output is the revisionist contention that America's industrial capitalists "were enterprisers, adventurers, and innovators, for the great forward strides of technology were possible only as a result of their risk-taking."[24] However, it was precisely the Robber Barons' role with respect to technology which led Veblen to term them saboteurs. The evidence that is available, scanty as it is, tends to support Veblen's view. The actual picture of the forward strides in technology reveals an extremely cautious exploitation of almost riskless opportunities.

Destler in his study of 43 capitalists found that at least 15 of the 38 nonbanking capitalists were alert to the advantage that adopting the latest technical improvements would give them in competition. Only three of those studied were inventors themselves, while another two used research technicians. As one

[20] R. M. Robertson, *History of the American Economy*, second ed. (New York, 1964), p. 418.
[21] See Robert E. Gallman's paper, "Commodity Output, 1839–1899," in *Studies in Income and Wealth*, Volume 24, National Bureau of Economic Research (Princeton, 1960), p. 37.

[22] Angus Maddison, *Economic Growth in the West: Comparative Experience in Europe and North America* (New York, 1964), p. 30.
[23] For Chinese growth, see United States Central Intelligence Agency, "Supplemental Statement," in *Comparisons of the United States and Soviet Economies*, Joint Economic Committee, 86th Congress, 2nd Session (Washington, D. C., 1960), p. 49.
[24] Louis M. Hacker, *American Capitalism, op. cit.*, p. 57.

major example, Standard Oil contributed nothing to the improvement of the basic technology of petroleum before the turn of the century. Destler concluded that "within the field of risks borne . . . the analysis indicates considerable success in exploitation of business opportunities involving little or no risk. Monopoly risk [i.e., no risk] was enjoyed by 21 in the group. Nine others profited from government subsidies or railroad-construction contracts, or both, that minimized the risks for the entrepreneurs involved."

Another relevant study was done by W. Paul Strassman, who examined four industries: iron and steel, textiles, machine tools, and electric power. His conclusions are radically different from those which revisionists would have us believe. He found that "the vast majority of innovations which seemed hazardous to people at the time were not, in fact, risky and that for most sweeping changes in manufacturing methods the process of innovation was already a safe and even predictable routine." This was due to the interrelatedness of innovations in key industries, so that change became mutually reinforcing. However, the pace of technological development "was not as rapid as might have been feasible on the basis of technology alone." Old methods of production managed to survive for decades after they became partially obsolete. For instance, in the textile industry ring spindles were a commercial success by 1845, but the number of mule spindles continued to increase until around 1900. Furthermore, more than ten years elapsed before the Northrop automatic loom appreciably reduced the sales of other looms. The same thing happened in the iron and steel industry: forges and bloomeries kept expanding after the introduction of puddling and rolling; charcoal smelting ex-

panded until around 1890; the number of puddling furnaces reached a maximum 25 years after Bessemer steel was successfully made in 1867; and crucible steel production increased for some 39 years after the first successful open hearth of 1870.[25] Strassman finds "conspicuous caution" as a major characteristic of entrepreneurs during this period.

CONCLUSION

We, see, then, that the final revisionist assertion, namely, that the Robber Barons were "adventurers" and risk-takers, falls under the weight of the facts. It has been shown that the revisionist arguments as to the critics, the state of popular discontent, the development of monopoly, and the creativity of the Robber Barons are all mere assertions, unsubstantiated by an examination of the available evidence. Matthew Josephson's terse description of the period still holds true: "The expanding America of the post-Civil War era was the paradise of freebooting capitalists, untrammeled and untaxed. . . . Theirs is the story of a well-nigh irresistible drive toward monopoly, which the plain citizens, Congresses, and Presidents opposed — seemingly in vain."

It is clear that the performance of the economy during the Gilded Age was poor. Yet, the revisionists are immune to facts. Thus, in the future we can expect to see more literature expounding the virtues of this or that capitalist, as the demand for such literature increases. And as the shortcomings of capitalism become more apparent, the demand for more and more baseless apologies will undoubtedly increase.

[25] W. Paul Strassman, *Risk and Technological Innovation* (Ithaca, 1958), pp. 19, 208, 216–217, *passim.*

Alfred D. Chandler, Jr.: NEITHER ROBBERS NOR BARONS, BUT BUSINESSMEN

Alfred D. Chandler, Jr. (1918–   ) was trained in history at Harvard, and taught at M.I.T. for many years before taking up his present professorship at Johns Hopkins in 1963. His most important work so far is Strategy and Structure *(1962), a breakthrough study of the administrative history of four giant firms (General Motors, DuPont, Standard Oil of New Jersey, and Sears, Roebuck), based on a wider examination of the history of about 100 American corporations. Chandler's intensive work not only tries to answer the historian's question:* How? *He goes beyond the amassing of historical evidence and descriptive details by placing his material in a theoretical framework to help us approach the question:* Why?*

The traditional Robber Baron concept has no place at all in Professor Chandler's work. He seeks neither to condemn nor to praise America's business leaders. He treats them simply as businessmen operating in a specific environment, determined by market conditions and structural economic changes.

BEFORE 1850 very few American businesses needed the services of a full-time administrator or required a clearly defined administrative structure. Industrial enterprises were very small, in comparison with those of today. And they were usually family affairs. The two or three men responsible for the destiny of a single enterprise handled all its basic activities — economic and administrative, operational and entrepreneurial. In the agrarian and commercial economy of ante-bellum America, business administration as a distinct activity did not yet exist. In mining, manufacturing, marketing, and even transportation, the largest firms were directed by a general superintendent and a president or treasurer. The general superintendent personally supervised the laboring force, whether miners, operators, engineers, conductors, or station agents. In the bigger textile and other manufacturing companies, the president or the treasurer usually handled the finances and arranged for the purchasing of materials and the sale of finished products from and to commissioned agents or other middlemen. On the railroad, the general superintendent carried on the commercial transactions of the company, setting rates, making contracts with shippers, buying materials and equipment, as well as scheduling trains and keeping track and equipment in good condition.

In the marketing and distribution of goods, merchants did most of their own buying and selling. When they were unable to carry on their business directly, they had agents who handled their accounts as well as those of other mercantile enterprises. If the amount of business was large enough, these agents sometimes became partners in the firm, particularly when the enterprise dealt with the transportation and sale of goods between distant commercial centers. Merchants, manufacturers, or railroad officers spent nearly all their time carrying on functional activities — the actual buying and selling or the personal supervision of the operations of a mill or a railroad. Only occasionally were they obliged to consider long-term plans such as the adoption of new machinery, taking on another line of merchandise, or the finding of a new partner or agent.

THE BEGINNINGS OF BUSINESS ADMINISTRATION IN THE UNITED STATES

Yet before 1850, a very few of the very largest American economic enterprises did develop embryonic administrative structures. John Jacob Astor's American Fur Company, Nicholas Biddle's Second Bank of the United States, and the state boards of public works or boards of directors of private corporations that built the major canals and first railroads, all these had field units and a headquarters. . . .

But with the completion of the great east-west trunk lines early in the 1850's administration became a full-time task in American business. The Erie, the New York Central, the Pennsylvania, the Baltimore & Ohio, and the western roads completed in that same decade, such as the Illinois Central, the Michigan Central, and the Michigan Southern, immediately became and long remained the largest business enterprises in the nation, and their operation demanded wholly new methods of management. . . .

As the roads grew in mileage and as their volume of traffic expanded rapidly, the number of their administrative personnel increased and their operating structure had to be redefined. The work involved in accounting and in the handling of passengers and freight grew so large as to call for separate offices for its supervision. At the same time, those activities related more directly to the movement of trains, such as the maintenance of way and of motive power and rolling stock, underwent a comparable departmentalization. Where McCallum of the Erie had innovated in the building of a structure for the administration of field units by departmental headquarters in the 1850's, the managers of the Pennsylvania Railroad pioneered in the 1860's and 1870's in working out a more extensive structure that defined the relations between departments. They spelled out the lines of communication and authority between the major and ancillary units within the transportation department and also between the transportation and the other major departments — the traffic and the accounting or financial departments. The Pennsylvania also created a central office group consisting of department heads who worked with the president to coordinate, appraise, and plan the activities of all the departments in the interest of the enterprise as a whole. Because they were full-time employees and had far more detailed knowledge, understanding, and information about the affairs of the road than the members of the board of directors, the president and the functional vice-presidents soon took over the making of long-term entrepreneurial decisions on the Pennsylvania and other railroads.

As the first private enterprises in the United States with modern administrative structures, the railroads provided industrialists with useful precedents for organization building when the industrial enterprises grew to be of comparable size and complexity. More than this, the building of the railroads, more than any other single factor, made possible this growth of the great industrial enterprise. By speedily enlarging the market for American manufacturing, mining, and marketing firms, the railroads permitted and, in fact, often required that these enterprises expand and subdivide their activities. Such subdivision or specialization, in turn, called for a concentration of effort on coordinating, appraising, and planning the work of the specialized units. Expanding markets also encouraged the use of more complex machinery in manufacturing establishments. This new and increasingly complicated machinery in turn spurred further increases in output and so provided another pressure for expansion and continued growth. . . .

In meeting the needs and seizing the opportunities created by the new national and increasingly urban market, many an American factory, mining, or marketing firm began to expand by multiplying the volume of output. Very quickly, these enterprises started to buy or build other units distant from their original locations. Soon, too, they were moving into new economic functions. These strategies of geographical dispersion and vertical integration had their beginnings before the depression of the 1870's dampened industrial growth for several years. Only after that depression, in the 1880's and early 1890's, did the great impersonal corporate enterprises appear in any numbers in American industry. Again during the 1890's a severe economic depression slowed growth. Then came the years of high prosperity after 1896 which saw the crest of the first great wave of industrial empire building in the United States. From the 1890's on, one of the basic challenges facing American industrialists was how to fashion the structures essential for the efficient administration of newly won

business empires. These enterprises, far too large to be managed by small family groups, came quickly to be administered by full-time professional managers. . . .

THE COMING OF THE INTEGRATED, MULTIDEPARTMENTAL ENTERPRISE

The coming of the first great integrated enterprises during the 1880's and 1890's brought entirely new problems of industrial management and led to the building of the first sizable administrative structures in American industry. The new administrative needs came less from an increase in volume of output than from the taking on of new functions. In the 1870's, nearly all American industrial enterprises only manufactured. They bought their supplies and sold their finished products through commissioned agents, wholesalers, and other middlemen. Mining enterprises operated in similar fashion; while mercantile firms nearly always handled a single activity, either retailing or wholesaling. By the end of the century, however, many American industries had become dominated by a few great enterprises that, besides manufacturing goods, sold them directly to retailers or even to the ultimate consumer, and purchased or even produced their own essential materials and other supplies. By now, too, a few merchandising companies were beginning to carry on both retail and wholesale functions, to buy directly from the manufacturer, and even to control manufacturing plants.

In manufacturing, the large multifunction enterprise sprang from two quite different strategies of growth. By one strategy, a single company began to expand and integrate through creating its own marketing organization. By the other, a number of manufacturing companies which had joined together in a horizontal combination — a trade association, pool, trust, or holding company — consolidated their manufacturing activities and then quickly moved forward into marketing or backward into purchasing. Firms making products based on new technological processes specifically for the growing urban markets usually found existing marketing channels unsatisfactory and so turned to the first of these strategies. The second type of strategy was employed much more often in industries producing the more staple commodities by an old and less complex technology. In these latter industries, expanded output often led to overproduction and then to combination. Both strategies were responses to the opportunities and pressures developing out of a rapidly growing national market. Both were also occasionally carried out by ambitious mining or marketing firms.

The story of Gustavus Swift provides an excellent example of an enterprise that grew through vertical integration by the creation of a marketing organization. A New England wholesale butcher, Swift moved to Chicago in the mid-1870's. Coming from Massachusetts, he was aware of the growing demand for fresh meat in the eastern cities. After the Civil War, Boston, New York, Philadelphia, and other urban areas were calling for much more meat than could be supplied locally. At the same time, great herds of cattle were gathering on the western plains. Swift saw an opportunity to bring together the new supply and the new demand by exploiting the new technology of refrigeration. In 1878, shortly after his first experimental shipment of refrigerated meat, he formed a partnership with his younger brother, Edwin, to market fresh western meat in the eastern cities.

For the next decade, Swift struggled hard to put into effect his plans for building a nationwide distributing and marketing organization. From the start, he realized that the refrigerated car could meet only part of his needs. There had to be a refrigerated storage plant or warehouse with a distributing and marketing organization in each major city. District offices or "branch houses," besides operating the warehouses, controlled wholesale and occasionally retail outlets in smaller towns and villages as well as in the major cities. Such outlets often came to be operated by Swift's own salaried representatives. The branch managers thus administered the different marketing activities within one area. By advertising and other means, they had to break down the prejudice against meat killed more than a thousand miles away and many weeks earlier and to defeat the concerted efforts of local butchers, who had recently created the National Butchers Protective Association to prevent the sale of fresh western meat in the eastern urban markets. At the same time, Swift had to combat the boycotts that the railroads had placed on his refrigerator cars.

By the end of the decade, Swift's initial strategies had proved eminently successful. His fast-growing distributing organization constantly called for more and more supplies. Between 1888 and 1892, Swift, who had incorporated his enterprise in 1885, set up meat-packing establishments in Omaha and St. Louis, and, after the depression of the 1900's, three more in St. Joseph, St. Paul, and Fort Worth. At the same time, the company systematized the buying of cattle and other products at the stockyards. It expanded its marketing facilities abroad as well as in the United States. Before the end of the 1890's, Swift had created a huge vertically integrated industrial empire.

Other packers quickly followed his example. To compete effectively, Armour, Morris, Cudahy, and Schwarzschild & Sulzberger had to build similarly integrated organizations. Those companies that did not follow the Swift model were destined to remain small, local ones. Thus, by the middle of the 1890's, with the rapid growth of these vertically integrated firms, the meat-packing industry had become oligopolistic. The "Big Five" had the major share of the market, each with its field units, functional departments, and central office.

Then, as each firm systematized the administration of its functional activities and devised techniques to coordinate the flow of products through the different departments, it also turned to developing goods that could further employ the vast resources it had collected. To beef, these firms quickly added a full line of meat products, including lamb, veal, and pork. To make better use of their branch-house network, they began to market poultry, eggs, and dairy products. To obtain more profit from their "disassembling" and other processing operations, they went into the leather, soap, fertilizer, and glue businesses.

The meat packers paid much less attention to the administration of their by-product operations than to their main line. Where the market for by-products was close to that for the primary products, the new businesses—such as poultry and eggs — were administered through the existing functional structure. Where the markets were very different, as in the case of leather and fertilizer, they were managed through subsidiaries or divisions to which the central office gave little direction. A senior executive was often responsible for a function and for

one or two by-products and, at the same time, helped to make strategic decisions for the enterprise as a whole.

In the same years, Swift's story was paralleled by other agricultural-processing industries whose products were destined for many urban consumers. In the tobacco industry, James B. Duke was the first to appreciate fully the growing market for cigarettes, a new product sold almost entirely in the cities. In 1881, he applied to the manufacturing of cigarettes a recently developed machine. Once he had adapted the new technology to the new demand, he concentrated on expanding his market by extensive advertising and by building up a national and international sales and distributing organization. By 1884, he had left Durham, North Carolina, for New York City, where he set up new factories, sales headquarters, and his central administrative offices. New York, closer to his markets, was a more logical place from which to run his world-wide industrial domain. As he continued to expand his distributing, marketing, and advertising organizations, he also set up a network of warehouses and purchasing offices in tobacco-growing areas. In 1890, Duke merged his company with five smaller concerns. Five years later, the activities of all these had been consolidated into the centralized, functionally departmentalized organization with marketing, manufacturing, purchasing, and financial departments that Duke had fashioned earlier. He then went on to obtain control, through purchases and mergers, of the producers of every other type of tobacco product except cigars. These later acquisitions were not all brought into the existing structure. Some remained integrated subsidiaries loosely administered from American Tobacco's offices at 111 Fifth Avenue.

What Duke and Swift did for their respective industries, James S. Bell and Andrew Preston did for flour and for bananas. In 1889 Bell took on the presidency of the Washburn-Crosby Company in Milwaukee and soon became known as "the greatest merchant miller in the world." He created a large marketing and distributing organization to sell to urban bakeries and retail stores high-grade flour made from spring wheat raised in the recently opened agricultural areas of the Northwest and processed by the new automatic-roller, gradual-reduction milling process. Similarly, in the banana industry, Preston fashioned the organization with its headquarters in Boston which in 1890 became the Boston Fruit Company and in 1899 the United Fruit Company. Preston, like Swift, made use of the new refrigerator technology in his ships, freight cars, and warehouses.

In developing new consumer durables, innovators also found it necessary to create their own marketing and distributing organizations. Both Cyrus McCormick, pioneer harvester manufacturer, and William Clark, the business brains of the Singer Sewing Machine Company, first sold their products through commission agents. Clark soon discovered, however, that salaried men working out of branch sales offices displayed, demonstrated, and serviced sewing machines more effectively and cheaply than did the agents. And just as important, the branch offices could provide the customer with essential credit. Then McCormick, while using the franchised dealer to handle the final sales, came to realize the need for a strong selling and distributing organization with warehouses, servicing facilities, and a large salaried force to stand behind the dealer. Thus in the years following

the Civil War, both the McCormick Reaper and the Singer Sewing Machine companies concentrated on building up first national and then world-wide sales departments. Since they purchased their raw materials from only a few industrial companies rather than from many individual farmers, their purchasing problems were less complex and required less attention than those of firms processing agricultural products. But the net result was the creation of a very similar type of organization.

Enterprises developing technologically advanced durable products for producers' markets also became dissatisfied with the existing sales channels. The most significant of these enterprises, in the 1880's, were in the new electrical field. Within a decade after Thomas Edison's proof of the practicality of an incandescent lighting system, two great corporations — General Electric and Westinghouse — came to dominate the industry. By that time, both firms were developing electrical machinery as a source of power for industrial and transportation businesses as well as for the generation of light. The marketing of electric lighting, power machinery, and traction equipment was so complicated technologically that it demanded highly trained salesmen who understood the power and transportation needs of their customers even more thoroughly than the customers themselves did. As the specifications for heavy equipment were very precise and varied with the needs of individual customers, the salesmen had to be in close contact with the manufacturing departments. Moreover, since the technological competition between the two firms was very intense, coordination between marketing, designing, and engineering personnel was essential.

The resulting departmental structure

reflected the types of markets in which the products were sold. General Electric and Westinghouse each had a manufacturing department to administer a number of scattered works or factories, a sales department to supervise a nationwide spread of district offices, an engineering department responsible for design, and a finance department. The sales and engineering headquarters included suboffices to handle the major products, for there were basic differences in the designing and marketing of heavy equipment and apparatus which were made to detailed customer specifications, such as large generators, motors, and switch gear, and lighter products which were made in volume ahead of orders, such as lamps, watt meters, and small motors and generators.

To some extent, steel manufacturers began to take over their own marketing because they too had technologically advanced products and an increasingly broadening market. Steel came to be produced on a large scale only in the 1870's, and at that time practically all the steel produced went into rails. In the next decade, as the basic railroad network was completed, structural steel for the new urban market became a major product. Carnegie's decision to use the steel produced at the Homestead works, one of the first great open-hearth works in the United States, for structures rather than rails symbolizes the change in both market and technology. Selling steel to contractors and builders as well as to the growing manufacturing companies in the machinery, agricultural-implement, and other industries required a larger sales force than selling to the relatively few railroads. As in the case of heavy electrical equipment, each order had its own specifications and so required close coordination between sales and manu-

facturing. Some companies also found it more satisfactory to distribute and market the more standard items made in advance of sale through their own "warehousing" organizations rather than through outsiders. As a result, the largest steel companies, like Carnegie, Illinois Steel, and Jones & Laughlin, by the 1890's had their own marketing organizations.

In the decade before the depression of the 1890's, Carnegie and apparently the other firms, had obtained control of their supplies of coke and coal, though not yet of ore. Most of the smaller makers of steel and those still manufacturing iron, however, remained essentially single-function enterprises, buying their raw materials from others and selling their products through middlemen. It should be noted, parenthetically, that the experience of the large electrical and steel companies was to provide examples for the organization builders at the du Pont Company, whereas the creators of the early automobile firms which became part of General Motors learned more from McCormick and Clark.

INTEGRATION VIA COMBINATION AND CONSOLIDATION

The more common road to the formation of the vertically integrated enterprise was by way of horizontal combination and consolidation. The threat of excess capacity appears to have been a primary stimulus to initial combinations in most American industries. But why did factories have difficulty in using fully their available resources in a period of swiftly growing markets? The answer seems to be that the rapid increase in the output of many small enterprises exceeded immediate demand. Each firm expanded because its executives hoped, particularly during the boom periods after the Civil War and again after the depression of the 1870's, to profit thereby from the new markets. Then, as the market became glutted and prices dropped, the many manufacturers became more and more willing to combine in order to control or limit competition by setting price and production schedules. So from the mid-1870's on, many small producers of leather, salt, sugar, whisky and other products made from corn, linseed and cotton oil, biscuit, fertilizer, petroleum, explosives, rope, and rubber joined in large horizontal combinations. Yet, such federations were usually short-lived. Production or price schedules were hard to enforce, even after the combinations became legal entities in the form of trusts or, after the passage of the New Jersey law in 1889, of holding companies. Another reason why they were unsuccessful was simply that they failed to employ fully and effectively the existing resources of their members.

Occasionally a federation dissolved into its original parts. More often it consolidated. And here the distinction between legal and administrative developments must be kept clear. The truly consolidated enterprise operating on a national scale required both new legal and new administrative forms. Legally, it called for an instrument that would permit it to operate in many different states. Administratively, it demanded a structure to provide for centralized coordination, appraisal, and planning for its extended plant and personnel.

Once the opportunity for nationwide operations appeared, the necessary legal instruments were not long in coming. The Standard Oil Company of Ohio formed the first trust in 1882, and by 1889 New Jersey had amended her general incorporation law to permit one corporation to purchase stock of another. Of these two legal innovations, the general incorporation law for holding companies was the most significant. Since the 1850's, railroads and occasionally other utilities (the American Bell Telephone Company, for example) had held stock in other companies, but such action was normally authorized by a special charter of incorporation, or an amendment to it, passed by a state legislature. Before the New Jersey amendment, no general incorporation law explicitly allowed a corporation to hold stock of other corporations. Some state laws, in fact, specifically forbade it. Moreover, many states penalized out-of-state corporations by prohibiting them from owning real estate in the state or subjecting them to special taxes. The provisions for general incorporation of holding companies, which other states soon borrowed from New Jersey, permitted a single parent company to hold the majority of the stock of locally chartered subsidiaries and so provided an inexpensive and easy way for enterprises operating over a wide area to avoid these obstacles and still to retain legal control over their geographically dispersed activities.

After the 1890's, administrative innovations were much more important to the development of American business than legal ones. A combination became administratively a consolidation only after its executive office began to do more than merely set price and production schedules. It remained a combination as long as decisions on how to produce or market and how to allocate resources for the present and in the future were left to the constituent enterprises. It became administratively consolidated when the small executive office was transformed into a centralized headquarters that determined nearly all the activities of the enterprise's plants or marketing units. The factories or sales offices, formerly managed by the heads of member firms, became operated by salaried plant managers or sales representatives.

The transformation of a loose alliance of manufacturing or marketing firms into a single consolidated organization with a central headquarters made possible economies of scale through standardization of processes and standardization in the procurement of materials. Of more significance, consolidation permitted a concentration of production in a few large favorably located factories. By handling a high volume of output, consolidated factories reduced the cost of making each individual unit. They could specialize further and subdivide the process of manufacturing and also were often able to develop and apply new technological improvements more easily than could smaller units. To a lesser extent, consolidations of marketing firms offered comparable advantages.

Horizontal consolidation and centralization immediately created much more pressure for vertical integration than did mere combination. The heavy fixed costs of enlarged plants or, in the case of a marketing firm, enlarged distribution facilities demanded a continuing high volume of output. A manufacturing company found it no longer safe to rely wholly on outside wholesalers or commission agents who also sold goods of competitors. The interests of these agents differed from those of the manufacturer. The wholesaler was often less concerned with increasing the volume necessary for reducing unit manufacturing costs than with obtaining a satisfactory "markup" or commission. He had no particular reason for pushing the

products of one client more than those of another. On the other hand, the manufacturer was unable to build up his own special market through brand names and advertising. Moreover, coordination between the marketers and the manufacturers and designers of products proved difficult. As a result, potential savings in cost were lost, and the development of products more nearly fitted to the customers' wants was inhibited. In time, too, many producers became convinced that they could distribute their wares more cheaply than their agents did. A manufacturer could assure himself of these advantages, however, only if his volume was large enough to support a national distributing system.

For these reasons, many consolidated firms, though certainly not all, began to do their own wholesaling and, occasionally, even retailing. They carried out this strategy by creating their own selling organizations or, more often, by combining with or buying existing large nationwide marketing enterprises. At the same time, many set up their own purchasing organizations. Only a few combinations, such as Standard Oil and United States Rubber, had embarked on this strategy of consolidation and integration before the depression of the 1890's. A much larger number did so in the years immediately following 1896. . . .

During these years, some enterprises went still further. Besides handling their own marketing and manufacturing, they took over the production — and often the transportation — of their raw materials. This expanded form of vertical integration usually occurred in those enterprises whose raw materials came out of the ground and where the limited supply could be controlled by a few firms. Such a situation posed the threat that the manufacturer would be unable to obtain his materials at a satisfactory price. Standard Oil moved into the production of crude oil in the late 1880's largely to gain an assured source of supply. In the late 1890's, the largest combinations, which became consolidations, in the fertilizer industry — the Virginia-Carolina Chemical Company and the American Agricultural Chemical Company — carried out a similar strategy for the same reasons. So too did a third fertilizer combination, the International Agricultural Corporation, somewhat later. After International Paper consolidated its mills and built its marketing organization, it purchased control of large tracts of timber in Maine and Canada.

Such defensive reasons played a particularly critical role in stimulating consolidation and integration in the iron and steel industries. The Carnegie Co., troubled by the concentration of control achieved during the depression of the 1890's in the Lake Superior iron-mining regions, purchased large holdings in the Mesabi Range. Other steel companies quickly followed suit. In 1898, Elbert H. Gary, with capital supplied by J. P. Morgan & Co., formed the Federal Steel Co., which combined Chicago's Illinois Steel Co. and the Lorain Steel Company (with plants in Lorain, Ohio, and Johnstown, Pennsylvania) with the Minnesota Iron Company. The new combination soon had railroads and a fleet of ore boats to provide transportation of the ore to the mills. In the same year, many small iron and steel firms in Ohio and Pennsylvania merged to form the Republic and National Steel Companies. Shortly thereafter, a similar combination in the Sault Sainte Marie area became the Lake Superior Corporation. These combinations began at once to consolidate their manufacturing activities, to set up their marketing organizations, and

to obtain control by lease and purchase of raw materials and transportation facilities. By 1900, several small firms making high-grade steel did much the same thing when they formed the Crucible Steel Company of America. About this time, the larger established steel companies like Jones & Laughlin, Lackawanna, and Cambria moved to obtain a more certain control over their supplies of ore and simultaneously altered their manufacturing or marketing organizations. Somewhat the same pattern can be discerned in the copper and other metals industries.

These combinations among the producers of semifinished steel and other metal products brought on, between 1898 and 1900, a wave of mergers among the users of steel, copper, and other semifinished materials. In addition to the threat of buying from a very few recently combined producers, who could set their own prices, the memories of unused capacity and low prices during the depression years of the 1890's and the persuasive arguments of the Wall Street promoters eager for the profits of combination stimulated these mergers. Among the users of iron, steel, and copper these included American Tin Plate, American Steel & Wire, American Steel Hoop, National Tube, American Bridge, American Sheet Steel, Shelby Steel Tube, American Can, National Enameling & Stamping Co., American Car & Foundry, American Locomotive, International Harvester, International Steam Pump, and American Brass Co. Some of these new enterprises were combinations of manufacturing works, but some like International Harvester, International Steam Pump, American Can, and American Brass were combinations of already consolidated, integrated companies.

Whatever their origin, most of these

combinations quickly consolidated their constituent companies into single operating organizations. Manufacturing facilities were unified and systematized, over-all accounting procedures instituted, and a national and often worldwide distributing organization formed. Some even began to assure themselves of control of supply by building their own rolling mills and blast furnaces. As the American Steel & Wire and National Tube began to make their own steel, they canceled contracts with Carnegie and other semifinished producers. This development, in turn, led Carnegie to bring forth plans to fabricate his own finished products.

The resulting threat of unemployed resources and price cutting led, as students of American business history know so well, to the formation of the United States Steel Corporation. This billion-dollar merger came to include the Carnegie, Federal, and National Steel companies, and the first six of the fabricating companies listed above. It continued as a combination. Although the activities of the various integrated, multifunction subsidiaries were re-formed and redefined, there was no over-all consolidation. Under the chairmanship of one of its most active founders, Elbert H. Gary, it remained, from an administrative standpoint, a federation of operating divisions loosely controlled by the holding company. Only in the 1930's, well after Gary's death, did the corporation's general offices at 71 Broadway begin effectively to coordinate, appraise, and plan policies and procedures for its numerous subsidiaries, and did so then only

after it had taken on a management structure very similar to the one Alfred P. Sloan had installed at General Motors many years earlier.

The years from the end of the depression of the 1870's until the turn of the century witnessed an enormous surge in American industrial output. By 1900, industrial capacity surpassed that of any other nation. During this same period of growth, the most dynamic and most significant of American industries had become dominated by a few great vertically integrated enterprises operating in national and often world markets. Small firms remained in these industries, but to exist they had to concentrate on a specialized product or meeting the needs of a local area.

In the last two decades of the nineteenth century, American industrialists concentrated their imagination and energy on the creation of these industrial empires. They became engrossed in planning the strategies of expansion and in securing the resources — the men, money, and equipment — necessary to meet the needs and challenges of a swiftly industrializing and urbanizing economy. The powerful captains — the Rockefellers, Swifts, Dukes, Garys, and Westinghouses — and their able lieutenants had little time and often little interest in fashioning a rational and systematic design for administering effectively the vast resources they had united under their control. Yet their strategies of expansion, consolidation, and integration demanded structural changes and innovations at all levels of administration.

Suggestions for Additional Reading

The Robber Barons, like everyone else, can be fully understood only within the setting of their own historical period. The difficulty is that their particular era is itself undergoing extensive reinterpretation by present-day revisionist historians. One recent collection of revisionist essays (though not especially revealing or iconoclastic) is *The Gilded Age: A Reappraisal,* ed. H. Wayne Morgan (Syracuse, 1963). Still more recent, and a thoroughly fresh look at the politics and alleged corruption of the Gilded Age is David Rothman's study of the Senate, *Politics and Power* (Cambridge, Mass., 1966).

Bearing all this in mind, anyone approaching the Robber Barons afresh should begin by reading one or two good but fairly orthodox narratives of the social and economic background. Outstanding are Edward C. Kirkland's *Industry Comes of Age, 1860–1897* (N. Y., 1961) and Harold U. Faulkner's *The Decline of Laissez-faire, 1897–1917* (N. Y., 1951) — Volumes 6 and 7 respectively of the ten-volume "Economic History of the United States" published by Holt, Rinehart and Winston. Graduate students and others will find full bibliographical guides to more advanced reading in both these narrative histories.

Peter d'A. Jones, *The Consumer Society: A History of American Capitalism* (N. Y., 1965, paperback) might prove useful as a general interpretation of U. S. economic history which tries to emphasize the sociological and economic factors without displacing entirely the part played by individuals including the great business leaders. Naturally, some knowledge of economics helps our comprehension of the Robber Barons and their times. The trouble is that no single economics book — not even excellent texts like Paul Samuelson's *Economics: An Introductory Analysis,* 6th ed. (N. Y., 1964) — can give the student of history exactly what he needs. If one is determined to come to grips with the mysteries of stock-watering, or interlocking directorates, or long-and-short-haul provisions, there is no alternative but to seek the answers in specialized books. A good example is G. L. Leffler's *The Stock Market,* 3rd ed., rev. by L. C. Farwell (N. Y., 1963), Chapter 12 of which is admirably clear and succinct on the art of "short selling" and other Wall Street techniques sometimes adopted by the Robber Barons. Fortunately, the newer breed of business historians have done much to explain these mysteries for a wider public. In this respect T. C. Cochran's short but concise *The American Business System, A Historical Perspective, 1900–1950* (N. Y., 1962, paperback; previously published by Harvard) has proved of help to many students.

During the Robber Baron era itself the two chief critics of big business were Ida M. Tarbell in her *History of the Standard Oil Company* (N. Y., 1904; 2 vols.), and Henry Demarest Lloyd in *Wealth against Commonwealth,* (N. Y., 1894). For selections see pp. 1–9 and 47–57 in this volume. A useful, annotated short version of *Wealth against Commonwealth* is now available with an introduction by T. C. Cochran (Englewood Cliffs, 1963). Among the many Muckraking exposés, D. G. Phillips (1867–1911), *The Treason of the Senate* (N. Y., 1906), is a slashing attack on alleged corrupt links between businessmen, particularly railroad leaders, and politicians — a classic Muckraking document, with all the strengths and weaknesses that this implies (available through Academic Reprints, Stanford, Calif., 1954). Theodore Roosevelt's censure of "criminals of vast wealth" can be found in his *Autobiography* (N. Y., 1913), especially pp. 483–498. Daniel Aaron's *Men of Good Hope* has remained since its first appearance in 1951 much the best interpretive survey of the thought of the Progressive reformers (N. Y., 1961, paperback). Read Chapter V for a brilliant characterization of Henry Demarest Lloyd as "the genuine evangelical progressive." A full-length biography is Chester McA. Destler's *Henry Demarest Lloyd and the Empire of Reform* (Philadelphia, 1963).

Writings of the day *in favor of* the Robber Barons include those of Edward Atkinson (see pp. 10–14, above). A good biography of Atkinson was published by Harold F. Williamson in 1934: *Edward Atkinson, The Biography of an American Liberal, 1827–1905* (Old Corner Book Store, Inc., Boston). The sociologist William Graham Sumner (1840–1910) willingly provided a philosophy for the business élite, especially in his essay, "The Concentration of Wealth: its Economic Justification," first published in 1902. This and other pieces are to be found in the second volume of Sumner's *Essays*, ed. A. G. Keller and M. R. Davie (New Haven, 1934). Sumner's distinctly conservative Social Darwinism was buttressed by the eloquence of Andrew Carnegie, whose *The Gospel of Wealth and Other Timely Essays* (N. Y., 1900) has been reprinted with an introduction by Edward C. Kirkland (Cambridge, Mass., 1962). For John D. Rockefeller's brief self-defense see his *Random Reminiscences of Men and Events* (N. Y., 1937), and U. S. Industrial Commission, *An Inside View of Trusts*, Testimony of Members of the Standard Oil Company (N. Y., 1899; pages 375–384 contain Rockefeller's own testimony regarding rebates.) The character of Andrew Carnegie's *Autobiography* (N. Y., 1933 [1920]) is illustrated on pp. 15–18, above. That literary businessman, C. F. Adams (1835–1915), who as railroad president fell afoul of Jay Gould, expressed the ambiguity of his attitude towards business in *Chapters of Erie* (with Henry Adams; Boston, 1871). His own chapter on stock-watering, by the way, is a good explanation of that device (pp. 398–413).

Historians have divided over the Robber Barons issue in much the same way that contemporaries did. Historical writing is subject to fashion, and does reflect the preoccupations of the writer's own era. On the other hand a review of Robber Baron historiography reveals certain continuities — each generation has had its own critics and supporters of Big Business. For instance the depressed 1930's were not an unlikely background for the publication of Matthew Josephson's fairly critical *The Robber Barons* (N. Y., 1934; paperback, 1962; see above, pp. 30–38. But that decade also produced numerous more favorable studies of business leaders. John T. Flynn's *God's Gold* (N. Y., 1932) was the first book to portray Rockefeller as a human being, feeling pain at the bitter abuse he suffered from jealous and ignorant competitors. Also sympathetic were Burton J. Hendrick's *Life of Andrew Carnegie* (N. Y., 1932; 2 vols.) and W. T. Hutchinson's *Cyrus Hall McCormick* (N. Y., 1930, 1935; 2 vols.). Allan Nevins had already launched upon the business history aspect of his prolific career with *Abram S. Hewitt, with Some Account of Peter Cooper* (N. Y., 1935), while the first version of his two-volume study of Rockefeller, *John D. Rockefeller: The Heroic Age of American Enterprise* was to appear in 1940. Among economic historians, Henrietta M. Larson had published her scholarly *Jay Cooke: Private Banker* (Cambridge, 1936).

Not everyone was happy with the new school of "business history," which in its early days was excessively defensive. The dangers of this pro-business bias were ably described in Daniel Aaron's "Note on the Businessman and the Historian," *Antioch Review* (Winter, 1947–48), pp. 575–584. Throughout the 1940's and '50's other writers, including Chester McA. Destler and Matthew Josephson, continued to dissent from the growing trend favoring business. In 1944 Destler had a short, sharp, public conflict with Allan Nevins in a scholarly journal over the accuracy of Henry Demarest Lloyd's indictment of Standard Oil. See Destler, "'Wealth against Commonwealth,' 1894 and 1944," *American Historical Review*, Vol. L, No. 1 (Oct. 1944), pp. 49–69 and Nevins' letter to the Editor, Vol. L, No. 3, (April 1945), pp. 676–689. Ten years later Nevins also debated Josephson in the more popular *Saturday Review*, Vol.

XXXVII (Feb. 6, 1954), pp. 9–10, 44–46: "Should American History Be Rewritten?" — Nevins answering yes, and Josephson no. But the eulogy did not die as a literary form; Stewart Holbrook's *The Age of the Moguls* (N. Y., 1953) and John Chamberlain's *The Enterprising Americans* (N. Y., 1963) are witnesses to that. And the process of "revisionism" has finally reached the N.A.M. with A. K. Steigerwalt's *The National Association of Manufacturers, 1895–1914* (Ann Arbor, 1964).

Since World War II, economic historians, encouraged partly by the growth of entrepreneurial studies at Harvard, have sought to get closer to the historical businessman and understand how he thought and operated. A product of this attitude have been the works by Grodinsky and by Passer, illustrated above; the writings of Fritz Redlich, particularly his *History of American Business Leaders:* Vol. I: *Theory, Iron and Steel, Iron Ore Mining* (Ann Arbor, 1940); Vol. II: *The Molding of American Banking, 1781–1840* (N. Y., 1947); *1840–1910,* (N. Y., 1951); and scholarly books like R. W. and M. E. Hidy, *Pioneering in Big Business, 1882–1911* (N. Y., 1955), T. C. Cochran, *Railroad Leaders, 1845–1890: The Business Mind in Action* (Cambridge, Mass., 1953), and Edward C. Kirkland, *Dream and Thought in the Business Community, 1860–1900* (Ithaca, 1953). Kirkland specifically seeks to know what business leaders really thought. See also his article, "The Robber Barons Revisited," *American Historical Review,* LXVI (October 1960), pp. 68–73, and his published lectures, *Business in the Gilded Age* (Madison, Wis., 1952). Another much-anthologized article is T. C. Cochran's "The Legend of the Robber Barons," *Pennsylvania Magazine of History and Biography,* LXXIV, No. 3, July 1950. Fritz Redlich's "The Business Leader As a 'Daimonic' Figure," *American Journal of Economics and Sociology,* XII (January 1953 *et seq.;* 2 parts), goes beyond the Robber Baron idea altogether and seeks to establish a useful typology of the business leader, who is perforce both creative and destruc-

tive in his social role. A quite different attempt to build a typology is to be found in G. Heberton Evans, Jr., "A Century of Entrepreneurship in the United States. . . ," *Explorations in Entrepreneurial History,* X (December 1957). Chester McA. Destler's, "Entrepreneurship Among the Robber Barons: A Trial Balance," *Journal of Economic History,* Supplement, Vol. 6 (1946), is still another attempt at a group portrait, different from both Redlich and Evans.

I. G. Wyllie's article "Social Darwinism and the Businessman," *Proceedings of the American Philosophical Society,* Vol. 103, No. 5 (October 1959), underplays the role of ideas like Social Darwinism in business thought, emphasizing the businessman's heavy commitment to meet day-to-day problems of great immediacy. Professor Wyllie has also written an interesting book on the origins of the great business leaders, *The Self-Made Man in America: The Myth of Rags to Riches* (New Brunswick, N. J., 1954). Other studies in this area are W. Lloyd Warner and J. Abegglen, *Big Business Leaders in America* (N. Y., 1955; paperback, N. Y., 1963); F. W. Taussig and C. S. Joslyn, *American Business Leaders: a Study in Social Origins and Social Stratification* (N. Y., 1932); a number of journal articles including C. Wright Mills' "The American Business Elite: a Collective Portrait," Tasks of Economic History, *Journal of Economic History* (Supplement), VI (1946), pp. 28–49; and the more recent work of William Miller, exemplified by the selection on pp. 18–26, above, and collected with other essays in his *Men In Business, Essays on the Historical Role of the Entrepreneur* (Cambridge, Mass., 1952; paperback, N. Y., 1962). See also Mabel Newcomer, *The Big Business Executive; The Factors that Made Him: 1900–1950* (N. Y., 1955). Occupational mobility in general is discussed in S. M. Lipset and R. Bendix, *Social Mobility in Industrial Society* (Berkeley, 1962; paperback). These studies, of course, go much beyond the Robber Baron period of American history, as do C. Wright Mills, *White Collar* (N. Y., 1956; paperback), and Reinhard Bendix, *Work and Authority in Industry: Ideologies of Management in the Course of Industrialization* (N. Y., 1963; paperback). The last two offer creative ideas from the field of sociology and may throw new light on the phenomenon of business leadership in history.

Almost a manifesto was *Change and The Entrepreneur* (Cambridge, Mass., 1949). It contains pieces by Schumpeter, Leland H. Jenks, T. C. Cochran and others, and illustrates the use of sociological concepts like "role" in economic history. Cochran has also pulled together some of his essays in *The Inner Revolution: Essays on the Social Sciences in History* (N. Y., 1964; paperback). Chapters 4, 5, and 8 are of special interest to students of business leadership. But the chief exemplar of the new business history is undoubtedly Alfred D. Chandler, Jr., a selection from whose *Strategy and Structure: Chapters in the History of the American Industrial Enterprise* (Cambridge, Mass., 1962; paperback, N. Y., 1966) terminates the readings in this book.

Sigmund Diamond, *The Reputation of the American Businessman* (Cambridge, Mass., 1955) is an unusual study based largely on obituaries. Hal Bridges usefully surveys "The Robber Baron Concept in American History" in the *Business History Review*, Vol. XXXII, No. I (Spring 1958), while John Tipple turns the tables on the Muckraking critics by examining their own social origins in "The Anatomy of Prejudice: Origins of the Robber Baron Legends," *Business History Review*, Vol. XXXIII, No. 4 (Winter 1959). The same journal yields William Woodruff's call for a new vision in the treatment of business leaders by historians, "History and the Businessmen," *Business History Review*, Vol. XXX, No. 3 (September 1956). Marxist criticism of the Robber Barons and of their revisionist historians will be found in Herbert Aptheker's *Laureates of Imperialism* (N. Y., 1954). Allen Solganick's critical article, "The Robber Baron Concept and Its Revisionists," *Science and Society*, Vol. XXIX, No. 3 (Summer 1965), is our nineteenth selection in this reader. For a general pro-business manifesto, see *Capitalism and the Historians*, ed. F. S. Von Hayek (Chicago, 1954).

Not covered by our readings is the "cultural" aspect of the Robber Baron controversy — the question of their art collections, their Fifth Avenue palaces, and (where this applies) their great philanthropy. Thorstein Veblen's theory of "conspicuous consumption" can be found in his *Theory of the Leisure Class* (1899), of which a good paperback reprint with a brilliant essay by a latter-day Veblen, the late C. Wright Mills, is available (N. Y., 1953). The great Englishman H. G. Wells made some interesting comments on the artistic proclivities of the Robber Barons in his *The Future in America* (N. Y., 1906), Chapter VI. And a reading of Frederick Townsend Martin's *The Passing of the Idle Rich* (N. Y., 1911), written by a member of the "idle rich," should provide amusement if nothing more.